INDIAN HEALING

Shamanic Ceremonialism
in the Pacific Northwest
Today

by Wolfgang G. Jilek

HIPPOCRATES

H. W. Gillen

house

ISBN 0-88839-120-X
Copyright © 1982 Wolfgang G. Jilek

Fourth Printing 1992

Cataloging in Publication Data
Jilek, Wolfgang G., 1930 -
    Indian Healing
    Parts of this book previously published as: Salish
    Indian Mental Health and Culture Change. 1974.
    Originally issued in series: Cultures and Communities:
    Native Peoples.
    Bibliography: p. 162
    ISBN 0-88839-120-X
    1. Salishan Indians–Psychology.   2. Salishan Indians—
    Rites and ceremonies.   3. North American Indians—
    Psychology.   4. North American Indians—Rites and
    ceremonies.   5. Shamanism.   I. Title.   II. Title: Salish
    Indian Mental Health and Culture Change.
    E99.S21J54 1981   616.8'914   C81-091279-1

Editor: Margaret Campbell and Mitchell Barnes
Production/Design: Peter Burakoff
Layout: Peter Burakoff and Lisa Smedman
Typeset by: Lisa Smedman in Times Roman on an AM Varityper
Comp/Edit.

Photos by author unless otherwise indicated

Published simultaneously in Canada and the United States by

HANCOCK HOUSE PUBLISHERS LTD.
19313 Zero Avenue, Surrey, B.C. V4P 1M7

HANCOCK HOUSE PUBLISHERS
1431 Harrison Avenue, Blaine, WA 98230

Contents

Foreword 5

The Author 7

The Book 8

Chapter One: Introduction 9

Chapter Two: The Revival of Spirit Dancing in the Fraser
                Valley of British Columbia 17

Chapter Three: The Achievement of Altered States of Conscious-
                ness in the Salish Guardian Spirit Complex as
                Documented in Ethnographic Literature 22

Note on the Physiology and Psychology of Altered States of
Consciousness 22
Spirit Experience and Possession 30
Spirit Quest 36
Spirit Illness 40
Spirit Dance Initiation 44

Chapter Four: Contemporary Spirit Illness and Anomic Depres-
                sion 50

Note on Anomie and Relative Deprivation 50
Anomic Depression as Important Background Phenomenon
of Contemporary Spirit Illness 52
The Symptomatology of Contemporary Spirit Illness 56

Chapter Five: The Therapeutic Process of Contemporary
                Spirit Dance Initiation 64

Death and Rebirth—The Therapeutic Myth 64
Personality Depatterning and Reorientation 66
Indications for Initiation and Selection of Candidates 80
Costs and Risks 83

Chapter Six: Annual Winter Therapy 86

Occupational and Activity Therapy 88
Group Therapy 88
Cathartic Abreaction 90

Psychodrama 92
Direct Ego-Support 93
Physical Exercise..94

Chapter Seven: Therapeutic Effectiveness 96

Chapter Eight: From Psychohygienic Ritual to Ritual Psychotherapy 101

Chapter Nine: Modern Spirit Dancing as a Therapeutic Social
Movement..109

Chapter Ten: Anomic Depression: Why Indian People
Die 117

Chapter Eleven: Structure and Symbolism of Shamanic Healing 130

Structure and Symbolism of Spirit Dance Initiation 132
Structure and Symbolism of the Power Board Ceremonial 138
Structure and Symbolism of "Indian Doctoring"...............145
Structure and Symbolism of the sxwaixwe Ceremonial.....148
Structure and Symbolism of Shamanic Ceremonials in Salish
Culture 153

Chapter Twelve: Renaissance of North American Indian Ceremonialism 158

References 162

Glossary 179

Acknowledgments.. 182

Foreword

by Professor M. Bleuler, M.D.
Zurich, Switzerland

An essential concern of European literature has for centuries been the portrayal of "manners and customs of exotic peoples".

Wolfgang Jilek is certainly qualified to make a valuable contribution to this topic from his own experiences, for he not only observed the traditional customs of North American Indian peoples, but shared with them their sorrows and their rare joys in many years of his work as physician and psychiatrist. Together with his wife, Dr. Louise Jilek-Aall, he lived and worked among Indian groups who strive to preserve their cultural heritage despite the fact that their home area has increasingly been populated by Whites during the last 100 years.

Some years ago I travelled the North Pacific Coast together with the Jileks, visiting the beautiful homeland of the Salish, the Nootka, and the Kwakiutl Indian nations. I was intrigued by the rich symbolism of their oral traditions, the noble greatness of their art, the psychological wisdom of their elders, and I shall always treasure the memory of my encounter with them.

Jilek describes peak experiences and turning points in the social and individual lives of the Indian people. But his book offers more than a fascinating description of Indian customs. It amounts to a vivid appeal to pay due respect to the cultural traditions of non-Western peoples, more so than has been the practice for a long time. Jilek demonstrates the importance of such traditions for the development of the mind and for the well-being of the people. It is a matter of embarrassment for our Western society that traditions of other cultures have often been looked down upon with condescension as the curious behavioural oddities of underdeveloped people who should learn something from us—rather than we from them. Such an attitude endured well into this century, often with inhuman, terrible consequences. Frequent attempts were made to suppress the ceremonial life of the Indian people by legal sanction and coercion. Jilek demonstrates that traditional customs have decisive significance for the Indian people's self esteem, for their enjoyment of living, and indeed for their will to live. He demonstrates that there is a necessary function of traditional customs in the service of the Indian people's mental health and survival, today more than ever before.

Moreover, Jilek shows that traditional customs are not only beneficial and necessary for the Indian people; we in Western society may learn a great deal by trying to understand the nature of these customs. True, the writers of Western schools of psychotherapy have taken up and presented ideas from Asian cultures, but they often also yielded to the temptation of ascribing to Western theories of psychotherapy a validity more general than warranted, transcending the limits of our culture area. On the other hand, we rarely feel called upon to learn from the psychotherapeutic experiences of Amerindian or African cultures. Jilek shows this is possible.

I have known Wolfgang Jilek and Louise Jilek-Aall since they both trained with us in Zurich as young physicians. We have seen them go beyond the borders of our country and it is with joy and with appreciation that we see them reach beyond the frontiers of our usual way of thinking and practice to make some new truths known to us.

M. Bleuler.

6

The Author

Wolfgang Jilek received his medical education in Vienna, Innsbruck, Munich, and Chicago. He trained as psychiatrist in hospitals affiliated with the medical schools of the Universities of Vienna, Zúrich, New York State, McGill, and the Université de Montréal; and did graduate studies in anthropology and sociology at McGill and the University of British Columbia. His degrees include an M.D. from the University of Innsbruck, a M.Sc. in Social Psychiatry from McGill, and a M.A. in Social Anthropology from the University of British Columbia. Dr. Jilek is Fellow of the Royal College of Physicians and Surgeons, Canada, a member of the Board of Advisors of the Transcultural Psychiatric Research Review, McGill University, Montreal, and of the Journal for Interdisciplinary Research "Ethnomedicine", Hamburg. In recent years he has been active as Chairman of the Section on Native Peoples' Mental Health, Canadian Psychiatric Association, organizing transcultural workshops in which Indian representatives from Canada and the United States participated together with health professionals. Dr. Jilek has done clinical research on chronic psychoses and neuroses, and on epilepsy. Together with his wife, Dr. Louise Jilek-Aall, who is a psychiatrist, anthropologist, and specialist in tropical medicine, he has conducted ethnopsychiatric investigations in East Africa, Haiti, South America, Thailand, Papua New Guinea, and Western Canada. Their contributions have been published in English, French, Spanish and German. After years of community psychiatric work in the Fraser Valley of British Columbia they are now residing near Vancouver where Dr. Jilek is Clinical Professor in the Department of Psychiatry, and Research Affiliate of the Department of Anthropology and Sociology, University of British Columbia. As consultant in the Psychiatric Outreach Program of the University he remains in close contact with the Indian people of the Pacific Northwest.

7

The Book

The guardian spirit ceremonial of the Coast Salish Indians combines the spirit quest of the Plateau tribes with the rich ceremonial life of Northwest Coast cultures. In this book, the author draws upon personal observations and upon information obtained in years of close contact with the Coast Salish people as physician and psychiatrist, as well as upon ethnographic literature. He witnessed the revival of the ceremonial after decades of suppression, and shows that, besides its complex traditional functions, it now provides the local native population with an annual winter treatment program in which several types of well-defined therapeutic procedures are integrated. These procedures compare favourably with Western medical management of psychophysiologic conditions and with Western correctional measures in behaviour disorders. Initiation into spirit dancing permits an alienated Indian person, suffering from what the author describes as *anomic depression*, to reidentify with the culture of his ancestors and to obtain the traditional guardian spirit power in order to grow with it into a more rewarding and healthier existence. In presenting a scientific analysis of the ceremonial, the author aims at dispelling misconceptions and negative opinions. It is hoped that the Indian elders and healers who have generously shared their knowledge with the author will be encouraged by this book to continue their efforts in the service of the Indian people.

Chapter One

Introduction

The "Guardian Spirit Complex" is an ancient phenomenon of considerable cultural, social and psychological significance for the great majority of indigenous American societies. Early European commentators considered the American Indian's guardian spirits to be daemons of infernal provenance. So did Bishop De Herrera in the sixteenth century, the Jesuit Fathers in the seventeenth century (Benedict 1923) and also Bishop Durieu of British Columbia in the late 1800s (Hill-Tout 1902); the latter identified them as familiar spirits.[1] The young science of anthropology was making the guardian spirit a case of totemism, either as an integral part of collective totemism (Durkheim 1915) or, *vice-versa*, as a universal precursor of totemism, a link between fetish and totem. (Hill-Tout 1901, 1904, 1905) More recently, clarifying reviews of the Guardian Spirit concept were presented for the whole of North America by Benedict (1923); for the Plateau area, including the Interior Salish, by Ray (1939); and for the Coast Salish by Barnett (1938, 1955) and Duff (1952). In comparative analysis of the Guardian Spirit Complex, these authors contrast Salish patterns with the peculiar forms this complex had developed among the Kwakiutl. (cf. Spradley 1963)

Generalizing from their conclusions, we see the following picture emerging with regard to Guardian Spirit practices in the Plateau and Northwest Coast culture areas:

(1) Prototypical of the Guardian Spirit customs is the Plateau area with an individual, egalitarian, rather stressful adolescent quest to obtain a life-long supernatural helper and acquire from him name, power, and song in a visionary experience.

(2) Contrasting with this is the situation in the Wakashan province of the Northwest Coast area with the Kwakiutl as prototype: highly formalized procedures, in which the Guardian Spirit as a mark of aristocratic rank is acquired on the basis of hierarchical principles in a dramatically staged group

performance of spirit vision and possession in the context of secret-society initiation.

(3) The Coast Salish area, in an intermediate position both geographically and culturally, manifests the Guardian Spirit Complex of the Plateau "re-worked and re-interpreted under the influence of the social and physical environment of the Northwest Coast" (Duff 1952: 111), combining elements of the classic spirit quest with the secret-society feature of initiation to the winter ceremonials.[2]

In Salish culture the most intimate relationship existed between shamanism and guardian spirit doctrine. Shamanism was, as Benedict (1923: 67) put it, "built around the vision-guardian-spirit complex". The following schema can be constructed for the Salish-speaking peoples from ethnographic literature (Teit 1900; Hill-Tout 1905a; Gunther 1927; Haeberlin 1930; Ray 1932; Olson 1936; Barnett 1938, 1955; Wike 1941; Duff 1952; Lane 1953; Jenness 1955; Elmendorf 1960; Robinson 1963; Kew 1970):

(1) Shamanistic powers and spirit-songs differed essentially from those of the layman. This distinction was carried to its logical extreme by the Upper Stalo of the Fraser Valley; their prospective shamans "underwent a long rigorous quest and obtained from a spirit in a dream or vision a specific power", while the same guardian spirit might appear to a lay person in a vision without quest, conferring no powers other than song and dance. (Duff 1952: 97)

(2) The shaman's spirit quest, although taking a similar form, generally implied greater efforts, imposed more hardships, and was of a longer duration than that of the layman.

(3) The shaman's vision experience was of greater force and intensity than the layman's.

(4) Shamans' and laymen's guardian spirits were, as a rule, of the same type or even identical, conferring shamanic powers to one and non-shamanic powers to another seeker. Shamans usually obtained powers not from one or two, but from several spirits, and often from spirits considered to be especially potent or to have predilection for shamanic powers. A notable exception was presented by Puget Sound groups (Haeberlin 1930; Wike 1941; Elmendorf 1960) having two

distinct classes of spirits for shaman and layman; and by the Nanaimo of Vancouver Island (Robinson 1963) whose shamans-to-be claimed mythical monsters as tutelaries while lay seekers had to resort to animal spirits. Barnett (1955) lists some spirits who gave power almost exclusively to shamans among the Coast Salish of British Columbia, such as the double-headed snake, the thunder-bird, the fire, and the land-otter.

The winter spirit dance was the major ritual within the guardian spirit complex of Salish-speaking peoples of the North-west Coast area. Spirit dancing was practiced by most Coast Salish groups that maintained effective inter-tribal ties through this ceremonial complex. (Suttles 1963) It was also of great importance to the Flathead as "medicine-dance," and to the Okanagan (Teit 1930), but by 1954 it had become a remnant of a once highly developed artistic and religious spectacle. (Lerman 1954) Spirit dancing was never a feature of ritual life among the other Interior Salish groups of British Columbia (Ray 1939); however, the Shuswap traditionally engaged in "mystery singing" during wintertime, when all men were possessed of some shamanic power. (Teit 1905)

The Salish Indians recognized winter as the appropriate time for ceremonies concerning the guardian spirits, when "people draw upon their store of sunlight and their vitality is weakened" (Robinson 1963), to be strengthened again by the annual return of the spirit powers who arrive and depart with the cold season.

In Hill-Tout's time (1902, 1904), the winter spirit ceremonials were known among the Halkomelem speakers of the Fraser Valley of British Columbia as *su'lia* or *úlia* dances, "dramatizations of dreams" as Hill-Tout (1904) interpreted this.[3] Today, the native population of the Valley refers to them in English as "Indian Dances", or just as "pow-wows". Under missionary influence, spirit dancing had to yield to Christian customs throughout the Salish region. Bishop Durieu who imposed a theocratic social order on the Gulf of Georgia Salish in the 1860s and 1870s, proclaimed four commandments to his Indian flock. The first was to give up all traditional dancing, the second, to quit potlatching, the third, to cease consulting shamans, and the fourth, to abstain from drinking and gambling. (Lemert 1955)

11

INDIAN BANDS WITH LINGUISTIC AFFILIATIONS

SALISHAN

Bc — Bella Coola
Cox — Comox
Co — Cowichan
Li — Lillooet
Nt — Ntlakyapamuk
Ok — Okanagan
Pu — Puntlatch
See — Seechelt
Se — Semiahmoo
Sh — Shuswap
So — Songish
Sq — Squamish

WAKASHAN

Hal — Haisla
He — Heiltsuk
Kw — Kwakiutl
Noo— Nootka

LEGEND

MAJOR LINGUISTIC GROUPS

CONTEMPORARY
Location and Population

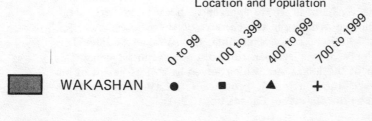

	0 to 99	100 to 399	400 to 699	700 to 1999
WAKASHAN	●	■	▲	+
SALISHAN	●	■	▲	+

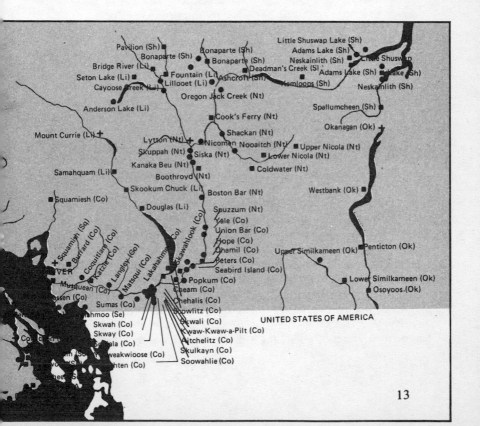

Little Shuswap Lake (Sh)
Pavilion (Sh)
Bonaparte (Sh)
Bonaparte (Sh)
Bonaparte (Sh)
Adams Lake (Sh)
Neskainlith (Sh)
Little Shuswap
Bridge River (Li)
Deadman's Creek (Sl)
Lake (Sh)
Seton Lake (Li)
Fountain (Li)
Ashcroft (Sh)
Adams Lake (Sh)
Lillooet (Li)
Kemloops (Sh)
Neskainlith (Sh)
Cayoose Creek (Li)
Oregon Jack Creek (Nt)
Anderson Lake (Li)
Spallumcheen (Sh)
Cook's Ferry (Nt)
Okanagan (Ok)
Mount Currie (Li)
Shackan (Nt)
Lytton (Nt)
Nicomen Nooaitch (Nt)
Upper Nicola (Nt)
Skuppah (Nt)
Siska (Nt)
Lower Nicola (Nt)
Kanaka Beu (Nt)
Samahquam (Li)
Boothroyd (Nt)
Coldwater (Nt)
Skookum Chuck (Li)
Boston Bar (Nt)
Westbank (Ok)
Squamiesh (Co)
Douglas (Li)
Spuzzum (Nt)
Yale (Co)
Union Bar (Co)
Hope (Co)
Upper Similkameen (Ok)
Penticton (Ok)
Burrard (Co)
Chamil (Co)
Squamish (Sq)
Coquitlam (Co)
Peters (Co)
Katzie (Co)
Langley (Co)
Seabird Island (Co)
VER
Matsqui (Co)
Lakahahmn
Lower Similkameen (Ok)
Musquean (Co)
Popkum (Co)
Osoyoos (Ok)
essen (Co)
Cheam (Co)
Sumas (Co)
Chehalis (Co)
hmoo (Se)
Scowlitz (Co)
Skwah (Co)
Skwali (Co)
Skway (Co)
Kwaw-Kwaw-a-Pilt (Co)
UNITED STATES OF AMERICA
Co
ala (Co)
Aitchelitz (Co)
weakwioose (Co)
Skulkayn (Co)
hten (Co)
Soowahlie (Co)

13

Initially there was no prospect of co-existence between Christianity and the spirit ceremonial. However, a seasonal pattern of religious loyalty developed later on in the Puget Sound with spirit singing in the winter and attendance at the syncretistic Shaker Church in summer. (Wike 1941) Spirit dancing was formally outlawed in Washington Territory by decree of the Superintendent of Indian Affairs in 1871, apparently because of fears about anti-White movements in the context of the Ghost Dance. (cf. Collins 1950) In British Columbia, the so-called Potlatch Law was often used as a legal sanction to suppress spirit dancing. This Section of the Indian Act, which served as an instrument of imposed acculturation in this province (cf. LaViolette 1961) remained on the Statutes of Canada until 1951:

> Every Indian or other person who engages in or assists in celebrating the Indian festival known as the 'Potlatch' or in the Indian dance known as the 'Tamanawas'[4] is guilty of a misdemeanour, and shall be liable to imprisonment for a term of not more than six nor less than two months in any gaol or other place of confinement, and any Indian or other person who encourages, either directly or indirectly, an Indian or Indians to get up such a festival or dance, or to celebrate the same, or who shall assist in the celebration of same, is guilty of a like offense, and shall be liable to the same punishment. (Section 3, Statutes of Canada, 1884; *op. cit.* La Violette 1961:43)

The history of spirit dancing among the Lummi, a Coast Salish group in Northern Washington, illustrates the development of the ceremonial under acculturative pressures. (Suttles 1954) Church and Indian Agency united forces to discourage this "pagan" ritual—paraphernalia and costumes were confiscated, their owners publicly chastised or sentenced to fines and forced labour if they proved recalcitrant dancers. Indoctrination at school was designed to make the young Indian generation consider the ceremonials as vestiges of a bygone age of barbarism. By 1914 the Indian Agent proudly declared the dances to be obsolete. When, however, he hit upon the idea of using them in a stage performance on "Treaty Day" for the purpose of arousing aversion, this had the paradoxical effect of rekindling a dying fire. It was now evident

14

to the people that the U.S. Government had finally been forced by the spirit powers to free the dances. There was, however, no resurgence of spirit dancing until much later.

While comparative data on most Coast Salish groups are discussed in this book, the population under specific observation here is that of the following Indian bands located in the Upper Fraser Valley of British Columbia (see map 1): Aitchelitz, Cheam, Chehalis, Kwaw-kwaw-a-pilt, Lakahahmen, Ohamil, Peters, Popkum, Scowlitz, Seabird Island, Skulkayn, Skwah, Skway, Soowahlie, Squiala, Sumas, Tzeachten, Yakweakwioose. They belong to the Halkomelem division of the Salishan linguistic group; Northwest Coast culture area. This region encompasses Indian reserves in the Greater Chilliwack-Agassiz-Harrison districts and will henceforth be referred to as Upper Stalo region. (cf. Duff, 1952) Also involved in the winter ceremonials of the Upper Stalo region are some members of the Douglas band of Northern Harrison Lake (Lillooet Salishan speakers of the Plateau culture area). The total Indian population of the Upper Stalo region amounts to about 2,000.

Footnotes

1. Spiritus familiaris, or imp, a low-ranking daemon in the shape of an animal given by the Devil to a witch or wizard with whom he had contracted a pact, to serve as advisor, assistant and performer of malicious errands. (Robbins 1959:190)

2. Among the Fraser River Salish, the winter dancing season was called by the Kwakiutl word Mé'itla according to Boas (1894). The contemporary Halkomelem term is mí. ɫ æ, to winterdance.

3. Cf. Kluckhohn's general theory of myths and rituals: "The literature is replete with instances of persons 'dreaming' that supernaturals summoned them, conducted them on travels or adventures, and finally admonished them thereafter to carry out certain rites . . . To obtain ceremony through dream is, of course, itself a pattern, a proper traditional way of obtaining a ceremony or power." (1942:51)

15

4. i.e., the spirit dance ceremonial; from *Tomanoas*, the gloss given as "Cowitchan" term for *guardian spirit* by Capt. Wilson (1866:281) who during his duties with the Boundary Commission 1858-60 obtained firsthand information on the Coast Salish spirit quest.

Chapter Two

The Revival of Spirit Dancing in the Fraser Valley of British Columbia

Among the Upper Stalo Salish of the Fraser Valley, Duff found only 14 active dancers in 1952. Ten years later, 26 new dancers were initiated during one winter in the entire Coast Salish region (Suttles 1963) Kew (1970) recorded eleven initiations at Musqueam Reserve near Vancouver in just three seasons, 1966 to 1969. Our data show that resurgence of spirit dancing on the Indian reserves of the Upper Stalo region started in 1967-68 with the initiation by Musqueam ritualists of the son of a prominent family, a young man of 20 years, who later was to assume a leading role in local initiatory procedures. In the mid-1960s, there were very few traditional dancers active in the Upper Stalo region (probably not more than four) of whom the most well known were Chief Richard Malloway of Sardis, and Chief Charles Douglas Senior of Rosedale. The legal persecution of active dancers under the Potlatch Law is still remembered among the older people, and so are presentations to the senior governments made by Chief Malloway and other Indian leaders on behalf of native traditions and of those practicing them. Throughout the period of suppression of spirit dancing by governmental and church authorities, the mutual assistance of the traditional dancers from different tribes who sang and drummed for each other, testifies to Salish solidarity. The few active dancers in the Upper Stalo region remained in close contact with their brethren of the Musqueam, Lummi (Northern Washington) and Cowichan (Vancouver Island) tribes, where the ceremonial had survived as an organized group activity. The leading role of Lummi and Musqueam ritualists in the revival of spirit dancing in the Upper Stalo region is readily acknowledged by local Indian leaders:

> It started in the States again, and it came this way; (C.L.);
> As far as initiation goes, Musqueam has been like a mother
> to the Chilliwack people . . . we had to depend on the other

tribes to help us, to teach us the Indian way of life again.
(Y.I.)

Indian leaders are aware of the historical importance of the revival of spirit dancing in the Upper Stalo region, and pay tribute to the role of ritualists of neighbouring tribes who from the mid-1960s on were practicing in the southern Coast Salish area:

> This is a great thing what happened here on our reserve, history has been made here. We are so grateful to our brothers from the South, from Lummi and from Musqueam and to Ed Brown [senior ritualist] who came all the way from Nanaimo . . . we'll always remember that. (Address at first ceremony on Wellington Reserve, December 23, 1970)

At the opening ceremonies of the new longhouse at Tzeachten, Sardis, B.C., January 8th and 9th, 1971, we counted approximately 800 people who had come from virtually all Coast Salish regions, as active or passive participants in the dances. To honour the historical event, *Sxwaixwe* masks and costumes were publicly displayed in a spirit dance ceremonial for the first time in many decades. *Four sxwaixwe* dancers appeared dancing *four* times around the hall, their accelerating pace "tamed" by the rhythmic drumming of *sixteen* traditionally clad older women.[1] The awe-inspiring ceremony was announced by a senior ritualist:

> Everyone off the floor now—*syə'wən* is coming out for the first time . . . let's the women hear, they're the ones that they're going to follow with their steps . . . It was in 1892 when this last took place, when they showed *sxwaixwe* here . . . Those of Chilliwack, Tzeachten is your home here, that's our way of opening it, our own way that we use to open this house.

The increasing number of "new dancers" in the Upper Stalo region not only reflects the proselytizing endeavour of the older ritualists, but also a changing view of native tradition by the younger Indian generations. Under the headline *Long House to Play Role in Reviving Indian Religion*, the local paper devoted a

18

full page to the revival of Indian Spirit ceremonials in the area, from which we quote relevant passages:

> Mrs. Point and her husband Roy described the current revival of interest in Indian beliefs and religious ceremonies ... Beliefs and practices which were uniquely Indian, began to die out when white missionaries moved into the area, she said ... Mrs. Point said that early Christian missionaries used various means to have native people drop their old beliefs ... She noted that with the completion of the longhouse, Chilliwack area Indians will be able to start practicing winter ceremonial spirit dancing ... Mrs. Point paid tribute to the role which Chief Malloway has played in 'keeping the fire burning' so that native traditions would not be lost ... She noted that many of the young native people who have dropped out of religious activities in the established churches are looking forward to the completion of the longhouse so that they can become involved in ceremonial dancing ... She noted that in attempting to restore the winter ceremonies, the people were relying somewhat on the rituals used by the more 'ferocious' Island initiators ... (The Chilliwack Progress, July 8, 1970:3B.)

These are the number of "new dancers" from reserves of the Upper Stalo region whom we were able to identify *ad personam:*

Initiated during *syə'wən* season:

1967-68 :   1
1968-69 :   3
1969-70 :   4
1970-71 : 16
1971-72 : 10

These figures are fairly complete; however, there may have been a few initiations which escaped our notice. Fifty would be a rather accurate estimate of the total number of spirit dancers in the Upper Stalo region who have been initiated since the revival of the winter ceremonials up to March, 1972. The drop in initiations during the 1971-72 season was not due to a lack of candidates, as

19

we could verify, but rather to a deliberate effort on the part of the new initiators to limit the number of novices, in order to "initiate them decent, so that they can better stand that way of life" (father of young initiator). According to Musqueam and Lummi ritualists, the trend towards increasing participation in the winter ceremonials has also been present in other Coast Salish regions. At one "big dance" near Duncan, Vancouver Island, during the ceremonial season 1970-71, 45 "new dancers" in their traditional robes gathered from all over the Coast Salish area. Also indicative of the growing interest in reviving the winter ceremonials are the smokehouse[2] construction projects which have been started by Coast Salish groups in recent years both in British Columbia (for example, Musqueam, North Vancouver, Duncan, Tzeachten, Chehalis) and in Washington State (for example, LaConner, Nooksack, Tulalip).

The revival of spirit dancing has been accompanied by changes in the ceremonial and in its organization, which will be discussed later. Most noticeable is the singing of spirit songs without text, and the use of English for important communications. Salishan tongues have become liturgical languages; their command accrues prestige to ceremonial speakers who will apologize for using English, "this foreign language". Such changes are viewed rather critically by some of the senior dancers and ritualists; others again accept them philosophically:

> Everything changes, syə'wən changes too, and it will change further in the future; but I know you'll keep the fires burning, and that's what counts. (Lummi ritualist at Tzeachten, January 8, 1971)

As a result of the scarcity of traditional dancers, the Upper Stalo region depended on the assistance of older ritualists from the Coast with regard to the initiation procedures. This is still the case in the Agassiz-Harrison area. In the Chilliwack district, a group of dynamic aspirant ritualists emerged from the ranks of those initiated in recent years. These young people devoted themselves to their ceremonial duties with great zeal during the season 1971-72, with only formal supervision by older ritualists. Even the most sympathetic elders watch their activity with some apprehension:

20

The young initiators are just starting and they have a lot to learn . . . they never used to allow anybody to do that if he was younger than maybe thirty. These boys are breaking into new territory. They are full of energy to initiate new dancers, but judging their experience I never trust it completely; something serious can happen during the initiation. (Y.I.)

Footnotes

1. Note the role of 4 and 4 x 4 as a quasi-magical number occurring in Salish ceremonial life. The *sxwaixwe* masks observed on this occasion were very similar to the Cowichan mask photographed 60 years ago by Curtis (1913:114); but obviously of recent manufacture. For the cultural implications of the *sxwaixwe* myth see Duff (1952), Barnett (1955), and Codere (1948). According to Chief Malloway of Sardis, the original *sxwaixwe* mask was fished out of Harrison River by two girls from Scowlitz, whose brother then displayed it on ceremonial occasions. The brother wore the feathers of this mask on the war path, which saved his life. Ever since, the Stalo people have carried feathers on their headdresses. One of the girls married into a Musqueam family and her rights to the mask were later passed on to heirs in Squamish. The other girl's rights went to Sumas where a priest eventually burnt all paraphernalia. Thus the Upper Stalo lost the mask, but the right to a *sxwaixwe* song is still claimed by Chief Malloway's family.

2. The terms "smokehouse", "longhouse" and "big house" are today used as equivalent designations for the wooden plank structures serving ceremonial functions in Coast Salish communities. The spacious hall is lined with rows of benches, of which sections are assigned to various tribes. The dancers move counterclockwise around the hall while three huge bonfires burn on the earth floor.

Chapter Three

The Achievement of Altered States of Consciousness in the Salish Guardian Spirit Complex as Documented in Ethnographic Literature

Note on the Physiology and Psychology of Altered States of Consciousness

To facilitate the interpretation of important phenomena occuring in Salish spirit quest and spirit dance initiation procedures, we present here a brief summary of the most relevant biological and psychological data on the genesis, character and function of altered states of consciousness. Ludwig (1968) has explored and described altered states of consciousness in the context of trance and possession. Altered states of consciousness are characterized by the following symptoms:

(1) alterations in thinking, including predominance of archaic modes of thought, blurring of cause-effect distinction, and cognitive ambivalence;

(2) disturbed time sense;

(3) loss of conscious control and inhibition which may be relinquished in order to gain a greater, culturally defined power;

(4) change in emotional expression towards affective extremes ranging from ecstasy to profound fear;

(5) body-image changes; feelings of depersonalization, derealization, dissolution of boundaries between self and environment, often associated with dizziness, weakness, blurred vision and analgesia;

(6) perceptual distortions; hallucinations, illusions, visual imagery, hyper-acuteness of perceptions, synaesthetic experiences;

(7) change in meaning; attachment of increased or specific significance to subjective experience or external cues, leading to thrilling feelings of insight, and revelation of "truth" which then carries an unshakeable conviction;

(8) sense of the ineffable; the essence of the personal experience

is felt to not be directly communicable, and this is often explained by varying degrees of amnesia;

(9) feelings of rejuvenation, of renewed hope or of rebirth;

(10) hypersuggestibility: a propensity to accept, or to respond uncritically to statements of an authority figure via identification, or to cultural and group expectations.

Ludwig's altered states of consciousness correspond to what Bleuler (1961) had defined as *Bewusstseinsverschiebung* (shifting of consciousness), a state of mind attributable to either cerebro-organic or, more frequently, to psychogenic processes. In Western culture, altered states of consciousness of a psychogenic type are mainly observed in (a) hypnosis, (b) religious revelation, (c) "hysterical" dissociation. The term *trance state* is in usage for all these phenomena, while *possession state* has been reserved for non-Western cultures and for cases not approved of by Christian authorities[1]—an arbitrary convention indicative of Eurocentric bias. The differences between these states are cultural, not psychological or neurophysiological. Schlesinger (1962) has accumulated evidence for a neuropsychological clarification of these hitherto vaguely defined experiences. His conclusions are briefly summarized here.

The term *trance* designates a "state of double consciousness, i.e., the constricted state of awareness of the personal self which co-exists with the dream-like state of consciousness of the para-personal self." The neuropsychological basis of any trance or possession state is the *dissociation of the self*, which loses its experiential unity and is converted into a secondary "dual system of relational experience," namely, the personal self and the para-personal self. A mild degree of dissociation of the central experiential agency involves the dominant or conscious sphere of mentation only; a more profound dissociation, the dominant and the subsidiary or unconscious sphere; and a maximal degree of dissociation would also effect cleavage of the mnemonic sphere, i.e. the memory functions.

There is no evidence of cerebro-organic changes as manifested in electroencephalography in either hypnotic or so-called hysterical trance states. (Lindsley 1960; Kugler 1966; Hill 1963 *op. cit.* Prince 1968) Some authors have found an inhibition of alpha-activity blocking under hypnosis. (Loomis *et al.* 1936; Titega and

23

Kluyskens 1962) EEG data of this kind which point to specific alterations of attention and consciousness were also obtained during Zen exercises in Japan. (Kasamatsu and Shimazono 1957; Kasamatsu and Hirai 1966)

The capacity of attaining altered states of consciousness is a universal property of the human central nervous system as evidenced by the ubiquitous occurrence of trance phenomena through time and space. However, the prevalence of these phenomena appears to be a function of socio-cultural variables. Under the impact of rationalistic-positivistic ideologies, the normal faculty of manifesting with psychogenic dissociation appears to have diminished among members of the Western urban middle class who would nowadays not be expected to readily enter hysterical twilight reactions, daemoniac possessions, or religious frenzy, while these states are by no means rare in more tradition-oriented pockets of Western culture (cf. Jilek and Jilek-Aall 1970).

Experimental studies of hypnotic trance have demonstrated beyond any doubt, (1) that the subject's motivation is essential for the induction of a hypnotic reaction; (2) that the hypnotist is of importance only as a culturally-approved sanctioning figure in whose influence the subject firmly believes, and as a focus for the projection of omnipotence fantasies; (3) that the hypnotic state serves the subject's wish-fulfillment and the achievement of consciously or unconsciously desired goals. (Schilder 1953; Barber 1958; Van der Walde 1965, 1968) Above all, hypnotic trance is a "product of situational and cultural demands." (Van der Walde 1968) This is equally true of non-experimental trance states. Paraphrasing the eminent French Psychiatrist Henri Ey,[2] we may say that in trance the subject makes use of his capacity to enter a dissociative state in order to enact most efficiently a goal-directed role which his culture in certain situations permits or demands him to do.

While the induction of psychogenic dissociation unquestionably depends on the subject's motivation, it may be facilitated by the employment of techniques which result in changes of brain function with demonstrable electroencephalographic indicators. Such "somato-psychological factors" (Ludwig 1968) producing altered states of consciousness are hypoxyventilation (inhaling air of low oxygen content) and hyperventilation (forced over-

24

breathing) which both can be carried on until loss of conscious-ness ensues, and which are associated with stage-specific EEG changes (Davis *et al.* 1938); further, hypoglycemia (low blood sugar level) and dehydration due to fasting; sleep deprivation; exposure to extreme temperatures. The role of rhythmic sensory stimulation in the production of altered states of consciousness deserves our special attention. While *photic driving*, i.e. the effects of stroboscopic photo-stimulation on electrical brain activity, perception and consciousness, has been the main concern of neurophysiological research in this field ever since the pio-neering work of Adrian and Matthews (1934), an analogous significance of acoustic stimulation has long been surmised by observers of rituals and ceremonies in which rhythmic sounds appeared to have a direct effect on the central nervous system. This was clearly expressed by Aldous Huxley (1961:369):

No man, however highly civilized, can listen for very long to African drumming, or Indian chanting, or Welsh hymn-singing, and retain intact his critical and self-conscious personality . . . if exposed long enough to the tom-toms and the singing, every one of our philosophers would end by capering and howling with the savages.

The well-known British neuropsychiatrist Sargant (1959:92) noted:

It should be more widely known that electrical recordings of the human brain show that it is particularly sensitive to rhythmic stimulation by percussion and bright light among other things and certain rates of rhythm can build up recordable abnormalities of brain function and explosive states of tension sufficient even to produce convulsive fits in predisposed subjects. Some people can be persuaded to dance in time with such rhythms until they collapse in exhaustion. Furthermore, it is easier to disorganize the normal function of the brain by attacking it simultaneously with several strong rhythms played in different tempos. This leads on to protective inhibition either rapidly in the weak inhibitory temperament or after a prolonged period of excitement in the strong excitatory one. Rhythmic drumming is found in the ceremonies of many primitive religions all over the world. The accompanying excitement and dancing is also maintained until the same point of physical and emotional collapse has been reached.

In their now classical treatise on rhythmic sensory stimulation, Walter and Grey Walter (1949:63) recorded the following physiological and psychological effects of such stimulation in their subjects:

1. Visual sensations with characters not present in the stimulus, that is: (a) Colour; (b) Pattern; (c) Movement.
2. Simple sensations in other than the visual mode: (a) Kinaesthetic (swaying, spinning, jumping, vertigo); (b) Cutaneous (tingling, pricking); (c) Auditory (rare); (d) Gustatory and olfactory (doubtful); (e) Visceral (probably connected with (a)).
3. General emotional and abstract experiences: (a) Fatigue; (b) Confusion; (c) Fear; (d) Disgust; (e) Anger; (f) Pleasure; (g) Disturbance of time sense.
4. Organized hallucinations of various types.
5. Clinical psychopathic states and epileptic seizures.

Although these effects were achieved by photic stimulation with rhythmically flickering light, the researchers had reason to assume that the mechanisms dealing with signals from non-visual sensory receptors were basically similar, and that "rhythmic stimulation in any mode is likely to produce impulse volleys at harmonic frequencies somewhere in the central nervous system, associated with specific illusory sensations." (1949:83) With regard to acoustic stimulation, they concluded that:

> ... rhythmic stimulation of the organ of hearing as a whole can be accomplished only by using a sound stimulus containing components of supra-liminal intensity over the whole gamut of audible frequencies—in effect a steep fronted sound such as that produced by an *untuned percussion instrument* or an explosion. (1949:82, italics mine)

This lead was not to be followed for some time. Instead of using rhythmic percussion, other researchers experimented with intermittent pure-tone sound stimulation, as, for example, Gastaut *et*

26

al. (1949) who elicited clinical responses in two patients suffering from photogenic epilepsy, and Goldman (1952) who could show "acoustic driving" in the EEG of two normal subjects. More recently, Kugler (1966) was able to elicit spikes in the EEG of patients suffering from temporal lobe epilepsy when using loud noises at a repetition rate of two to six per second. It was not until Neher's investigations (1960; 1962) that the neurophysiological effects of rhythmic drumming were demonstrated in controlled experiments. The significance of Neher's findings for the anthropological and psychological study of ritual trance and possession states can hardly be over-estimed. Neher (1960) exposed clinically and electroencephalographically normal subjects to a low-frequency, high-amplitude stimulus obtained from a snare drum without snares—an instrument quite similar to the Salish deer skin drums employed at winter ceremonials. *Auditory driving* responses were demonstrated in the EEG of all subjects at the fundamental of each stimulus frequency (three, four, six and eight beats per second), also at second harmonics and second subharmonics of some stimulus frequencies. Subjective responses were similar to those obtained with photic driving by Walter and Grey Walter (1949), and included "fear, astonishment, amusement, back pulsing, muscle tightening, stiffness in chest, tone in background, humming, rattling, visual and auditory imagery." Due to the presence of theta rhythms (four to seven cycles per second) in the electrical activity of the temporal auditory region of the cerebral cortex, sound stimulation by drumming in this frequency range appears to be most effective and would, therefore, be expected to predominate in ceremonies associated with trance behaviour. As cited by Neher (1962) the response is heightened by accompanying rhythms reinforcing the main rhythm, and by concomitant rhythmic stimulation in other sensory modes, such as tactual and kinesthetic; susceptibility to rhythmic stimulation is increased by stress in general, hyperventilation, hypoglycemia and adrenaline secretion resulting from exertion and fatigue. At the same time, strong sensory stimulation inhibits the transmission of pain signals to the conscious areas of the brain. In the light of his findings, Neher (1962) reviewed some ethnographic reports on ceremonies involving rhythmic drumming from Siberia, Africa, Haiti and Indonesia. A comparison of these data appeared to suggest that "unusual be-

27

haviour observed in drum ceremonies is mainly the result of rhythmic drumming which affects the central nervous system." However, such a conclusion awaits final confirmation by electro-encephalographic examination of subjects while participating in appropriate ceremonies. Prince (1968) discusses the possibility that auditory driving is a "commonly used portal of entry into the dissociative state." His practical suggestions for the study of possession states by telemetering the EEG of fully mobile "native" participants in ceremonies have not yet been taken up by field researchers.

Sargant (1959) explains the induction of states of religious enthusiasm and spirit possession, as well as the so-called brain-washing and related therapeutic techniques, in terms of Pavlovian theory as *transmarginal inhibition*. He marshals evidence from historical and contemporary reports on methods of religious and ideological conversion and indoctrination, and shows that the basic processes involved are analogous in all significant aspects, paralleling those Pavlov deduced from his experimental obser-vations in dogs. Given the fact that human cerebral organization varies within very narrow limits, we should not be surprised to find the most heterogenous ideologies introduced successfully by very similar techniques, as Sargant (1959:128) asserts:

> Various types of belief can be implanted in many people, after brain function has been sufficiently disturbed by accidentally or deliberately induced fear, anger or excite-ment. Of the results caused by such disturbances, the most common one is temporarily impaired judgement and heightened suggestibility . . . If a complete sudden collapse can be produced by prolonging or intensifying emotional stress, the brain slate may be wiped clean temporarily of its more recently implanted patterns of behaviour, perhaps allowing others to be substituted for them more easily.

Ludwig (1968) presents a classification of factors in the production of altered states of consciousness under the following headings:

28

a) reduction of external stimulation and/or motor activity: for example, in sensory deprivation, prolonged social isolation, hypnagogic and hypnopompic states, revelatory states during incubation or temple sleep;

b) increase of external stimulation and motor hyperactivity, emotional arousal leading to exertion and mental fatigue: for example, in hyperalert or hyperkinetic trance secondary to tension-induction manoeuvres; trance in response to rhythmic music and drumming; trance in revivalistic meetings or spirit possession in tribal ceremonies; increased suggestibility and sense-deceptions resulting from prolonged fear;

c) focused and selective hyperalertness: for example, in prolonged vigilance, intense mental absorption or attention to proprioceptive stimuli;

d) decreased alertness, relaxation of critical faculties: for example, in meditation, day-dreaming and reverie, auto-hypnotic trances;

e) somatopsychological factors *(vide supra)*.

From the foregoing we conclude that *trance* or *possession* are altered states of consciousness involving the universally human mechanism of mental dissociation without cerebro-organic lesions. Their induction is largely dependent on the subject's motivation and on the situational and socio-cultural context but may be facilitated by certain conditions and techniques, some of which effect temporary changes of brain function.

It may be appropriate here to raise the question of the functional relevance of altered states of consciousness for the individual and for the collective. This question has recently been answered by Wittkower (1970) in a discussion of his observations on trance and possession states in non-Western societies:

> Trance and possession states have undoubtedly an adaptive function culturally as well as individually. Their individual psychological effects consist of drive release, ego support, problem solution, relief from superego pressures and atonement.

> There can be no doubt in anybody's mind that trance and possession states in the countries in which they play part of religious rituals have an important distress relieving, inte-

grative, adaptive function. As far as mental illness is concerned, they may be of prophylactic value. An increase in mental illness may have to be expected when as a result of culture change they have ceased to exist.

Spirit Experience and Possession

Fundamental to the North American Guardian Spirit Complex is the vision experience as a means of obtaining and controlling supernatural power. (Benedict 1923) Tribal convention and formalization of the content of the vision and the events surrounding it cannot obscure the fact that this experience was distinguished from others by intense feelings of significance and "thrill", and that it constituted a specific psychic reaction which was socially recognized. The tutelaries were mostly acquired in a peri-pubertal spirit quest. They were usually seen and/or heard in a vision encounter and showed themselves to the power-seeker both in human and non-human form. After surveying the literature one will agree with Benedict (1923) that the Guardian Spirits were named entities recruited from a very wide range of the natural and supernatural universe, making it impossible to group them under any one type. In Benedict's view the North American Indian's vision experience was not synonymous with dreaming. Some authors quote informants as expressly referring to visions in a non-sleeping state, for example, Hill-Tout (1905:144) and Duff (1952:99). Robinson (1963) states for the Nanaimo of Vancouver Island that it was necessary to fall unconscious in order to hallucinate the tutelary and that sleep dreams were considered inadequate. Other authors are less specific and use vision and dream interchangeably. Thus, according to Barnett (1955), among the Coast Salish of British Columbia the "mystic rapprochement in which the seeker was granted the aid of an animal spirit always took place in a dream or trance." Teit (1900, 1905, 1930) speaks of "dreams" or of "dreams and visions" in connection with Guardian Spirit acquisition among the Thompson, Shuswap, and other Salishan tribes of the Plateau. He refers to the prototypical case of the Thompson when reporting that "the ceremonial rites continued until the lad dreamed of some animal or bird which became his protectors or Guardian Spirits for life." (Teit 1900:320) The Coast Salish youth's vision quest had to go

30

on until he eventually would "see something." (Barnett 1955)
"Dreams and visions are the invariable source of the personal
totem of the Salish" concludes Hill-Tout (1905:143). In his
writings Hill-Tout (1901, 1902, 1904, 1905a, 1905b, 1907) uses
labels like personal totem, guardian, mystery being, essence,
guide, tutelary, protector, power, charm, or fetish, for the
Halkomelem term *su'lia* which he dervies from the verb *u'lia* "to
dream". (Hill-Tout 1901, 1902) This etymology of the Halkomelem term for Guardian Spirit is confirmed by Duff (1952)
for the Upper Stalo—*su'lia*, meaning "dream" but possibly also
"vision" (*a'lia* "vision" or "prophet") denotes both the Guardian
Spirit experience and the Guardian Spirit; and by Kew (1970) for
the Musqueam —*s'ólyə*, literally one's vision or "what you see in
your dream". Suttles (1955) gives the translation of the identical
Katzie word as "vision". The analogous term in Twana language
was *s'ɑlixʷ*, "that which one encounters in a vision experience",
from *ɑli'xʷ*, "to obtain power from a Guardian Spirit in a vision-
encounter". The Twana made no sharp distinction between
waking vision, trance, or semi-conscious hallucination. It was
assumed that the seeker would have to "lose consciousness" as if
dying, in order to perceive the spirit in human form and be
granted power and song, upon which he would recover from a
"fainting spell." (Elmendorf 1960) The powers conferred by the
Guardian Spirit on the seeker in his vision experience are signified and/or embodied in the spirit song which in Halkomelem
languages was called *ši'wəl* (Duff 1952), *siɑ'wən* (Suttles 1955) or
syə'wən (Kew 1970).[3]

Ray (1932) assumes that the majority of guardian spirit
experiences among the Sanpoil and Nespelem were dream
phenomena, although sleep was not permitted on the quest and
the experience was spoken of as "like a dream". Later on in his
review of cultural relations in the Plateau, Ray (1939) points out
that this experience may take place in a "half-waking or half-
sleeping state and yet be culturally classified as definitely dream,
or definitely vision"—according to intra-group convention, as it
were. It appears to be quite plausible that the vision was elaborated in subsequent dreams, as Olson (1936) reports for the
Quinault youths seeking spirit power. This has a parallel in Lane's
(1953) findings in the Cowichan area of Vancouver Island where
visions occurred in either a conscious or unconscious state

followed by spirit appearance in dreams. Wike's (1941) accounts of the Swinomish of Puget Sound also refer to reappearance in sleep dream after initial perception of a spirit helper.

The dream-vision question remains unresolved, therefore, and may be unresolvable due to an inherent semantic ambivalence in the native concepts, an ambivalence which would seem to aptly express the ambivalent nature of altered states of consciousness partaking of properties of the sleep-dream and of normal wakefulness.

The Indian informants' accounts reflect the intensity of the psychophysiologic reaction experienced by the youthful spirit seeker in his first encounter with the supernatural:

> ... in the middle of the second night there came a roaring as of wind, things came through the air and the ground swayed and rocked. Then I heard the scream of an eagle. He came near and I saw him in the guise of a man. He went round and round the fire and then went away. I was very much afraid and wanted to run away. Then I heard the sea-monster nearby, and he, too, walked around me. I was afraid he was going to carry me off. Then there came a monster snake who made a noise like the land otter. Finally Turtle came and walked around me and went away. Each of them gave me power. (Quinault; Olson 1936:144)

> Four winters I endured this penance. Then at last my mind and body became really clean. My eyes were opened, and I beheld the whole universe. I had been dancing and had fallen to the ground exhausted. As I lay there, I heard a medicine-man singing far, far away, and my mind travelled towards the voice ... My mind returned to my body and I awoke, but now in my hands and wrists I felt power. I rose up and danced until I fell exhausted again and my mind left me once more. Now I travelled to a huge tree—the father of all trees, invisible to mortal eyes." (Katzie; Jenness 1955:67)

> The owl was so close. It was sitting down on a log. When I frightened it, it flew up on top of a tree. I don't know whether I fainted or not. When I got control I went home. That night I dreamed about it. It came up to me and talked

to me. (Swinomish; Wike 1941:15)

Comes the noise again just like a whirlwind, struck me on my back. I stopped and looked around. Funny, no wind or nothing. I walked again then. I seen lightning sparkle across the road. I just wondered, what was that? I looked up again, seen the stars. It couldn't be thunder. I went on the same and I was really hungry. Again it come, a little closer, whirled right across in front of me. It gave me chills through my body the second time it come. I kept a-walking. Finally the third time it come and got me, struck me on the right side, shot right into me. I kind of staggered, dropped onto my knees, fell over. This man come to me then, (and said) 'I'm the spirit that your great-grandfather had'; a great tall old man with long hair like a woman. (Swinomish; Wike 1941:18)

The spirit may be of immediate assistance, emotionally and materially, in situations of distress, as in the case of a deserted, deprived and depressed young Swinomish mother to whom the Deer Spirit restored hope and brought hunting luck:

One day after I ate lunch I lay in bed, 'Well, what is life? If I should only die I wouldn't have to worry about my little ones. But poor littles ones they need me.' Then that night I dreamed. I saw the little deer in my dream. I almost loved that little thing when I saw it. It said 'You are going to walk down this morning and carry a gun and you are going to meet me.' (Spirit then supplied psychic support together with material provisions for the family, Wike 1941:16)

After successful completion of the spirit quest the general pattern was to claim amnesia for, or at least to not reveal, details of the spirit encounter and of the powers obtained from the super-natural guardians until one was seized, perhaps years later, by the seasonal spirit sickness when the spirit song had to be "brought out" in either the spirit singing (Plateau) or the winter spirit dance ceremonials (Coast Salish).

The Twana present a prototypical example of the Southern Coast Salish guardian spirit complex. (Elmendorf 1960) The

33

guardian spirits, acquired in a vision quest, are later recalled and controlled during the winter dance season in a fixed sequence: the spirits return early in winter, manifesting themselves by the spirit illness (see below) which, when first afflicting a person several years after his spirit vision, has to be diagnosed by a shaman. From then on, the spirit returns annually to its human owner and is ceremonially exhibited during each dancing season. Seasonal possession upon return of the much earlier acquired spirit at maturity was also the pattern among three Interior Salish groups of the Plateau (Okanagan, Sanpoil, and Kalispel) and required shamanistic intervention to establish a relationship beneficial to the owner. (Ray 1939) However, spirit power might prove even too strong for a shaman to handle, as in the case of the officiating ritualist who collapsed in a possession state during an Okanagan Winter Dance. (Lerman 1954) In the Upper Fraser Valley, the traditional ways of acquiring the spirit song (ši'wǝl)—the individual guardian spirit power received by most of the Upper Stalo Indians—were (Duff 1952): (1) spirit song acquisition in a spontaneous seizure-like dream or vision experience; (2) acquisition in a fit induced by actions of older dancers; (3) song heard in an ordinary dream; (4) song heard emanating from natural objects. Spirit song acquisition of types (1) and (2) occurred only during the winter dancing time, while types (3) and (4) were not restricted to any season. The Musqueam in the Lower Fraser area (Kew 1970) also knew, and know, the alternative forms of spirit acquisition either through individual quest or through actions performed by other qualified spirit owners. The spiritual force (syǝ'wǝn) resides within the individual and is manifested in a "state of trance and seizure". The spirit-song, conferred in the first encounter with the supernatural, has to be sung every year during the ceremonial season. Subsequent to its first manifestation, possession by syǝ'wǝn may be triggered by hearing sudden noises or the singing of others. The triggering effect of any kind of music during the winter dance period is familiar to the Swinomish of Puget Sound. Genuine trance states in traditional Swinomish spirit dancers are indicated by violent sobbing, fainting, acute fatigue, or mad frenzy potentially leading to accidents, symptoms resembling the clinical picture of hysteria (Wike 1941) especially with regard to the anaesthetic and analgesic phenomena. The possessed dancer's movements appear as "puppet-like" automaton movements even to a casual observer. (Altman 1947) The immediacy of the possession experience is reflected in the accounts of the dancers:

> When you sing your breath starts shaking. After a while it goes into you. You try to sing, your jaws start to shake, then you sing it out, get over it. When I dance I don't act, just follow your power, just follow the way of your power.

> The spirit come right into me. Couldn't hold my breath, began to sing. When I dance the spirit is in me so strong. The song is going in my ear all the time. I'm not myself until it raises away from you, then it's clear . . . The spirit is so strong I can't stop. (Wike 1941:13,14)

Among the Lummi Indians, all persons who acquired spirit songs from their tutelaries between puberty and middle age, became possessed and sang during the winter season. (Suttles 1954) Of the Puyallup-Nisqually of Puget Sound, Smith (1940) reports that their newly possessed are in deep trance and appear like dead. Hill-Tout (1900:488) observed that the Squamish spirit dancer is "practically in a hypnotic trance state . . . moved or prompted by self-suggestion or the mental suggestion of the waiting audience." However, experienced Salish spirit dancers learn to exercise some control over their spirits and to determine to a certain extent the time of possession (Wike 1941), which is, of course, not at all incompatible with an altered state of consciousness. Spirit power, especially of the nascent song, is held to be highly contagious. (Barnett 1955; Kew 1970; Smith 1940; Stern 1934; Suttles 1963; Wike 1941)

Barnett (1955) has maintained that genuine possession was more common in the southern Coast Salish region, while in the North (Comox) it was either absent or pretended. That genuine possession states occurred among the Vancouver Island Salish, is confirmed by Lane's (1953) data on the Cowichan ("comatose" state of new dancers repossessed by their power, automatic singing and barking of the spirit dancers, etc.). Barnett's conclusion appears to be based on the fallacious assumption that the culturally conditioned expectation to enter into a trance state can only be complied with by conscious simulation:

On the island, at least, performers of the winter ceremonials were supposed to be possessed by their spirits, and this . . . indicates the pretense and artificiality entering into many of the winter ceremonials. (Barnett 1955:272)

Neuropsychological research has, however, long demonstrated the error of equating phenomena, brought about by collective suggestion, with "pretense and artificiality." An extreme but illustrative case in point is the phenomenon variously labelled *voodoo death, thanatomania, mort psychosomatique,* or *Vagus-Tod*; namely, the lethal outcome of severe anxiety states, anticipated by the afflicted individual as well as by its group, and induced and reinforced by the collective suggestion of supernatural influences. (cf. Ackerknecht 1943; Bilz 1966; Cannon 1942; Collomb 1965; Ellenberger 1951; Jilek-Aall 1964; Jilek and Jilek-Aall 1970; Lambo 1956; Mauss 1950)

Spirit Quest

We will now examine the conditions which played a major rôle in the production of altered states of consciousness in the traditional Salish guardian spirit quest.

Conditions of social isolation associated with prolonged nocturnal vigilance, expectant alertness, and monotony: The Thompson youth's practice extended over years which he spent periodically on lonely vigils in the mountains (Teit 1900), just as the Flathead had to keep vigil in desolate places. (Teit 1930) Shuswap boys separated themselves for weeks of nocturnal seclusion in wild spots. (Teit 1905) Vigils among the Lillooet might last up to one year (Ray 1939); the young seeker would go apart by himself into forest or mountains, trying to keep his mind abnormally active and expectant. (Hill-Tout 1905a, 1905b) On the Plateau, visions tended to be hypnagogic or hypnopompic hallucinations, preceding actual sleep or following awakening. (Ray 1939) Among the Coast Salish of B.C. it was the rule to go into the woods and stay alone in the wilderness. (Barnett 1938) Comox seekers were expected to remain away until they were believed to be dead. (Barnett 1955) Dozens of vigils in solitary places such as mountain tops were held by Sanpoil boys (Ray

36

1932); while the young Quinault had to maintain vigilance for several days after long trips in the mountains, up creeks, or on the shore in search of a suitable place for his vision. (Olson 1936) The Twana spirit seeker was sent out alone at night to remote locations (Elmendorf 1960) and the Swinomish had to walk by himself many miles through the forest. (Wike 1941) Repetitive praying and singing propitiated the spirits. (Teit 1900, 1930; Olson 1936) The seekers were advised to play solitary games all night such as going through the motions of playing *lahal* (for example, Ray 1932).

Conditions of motor hyperactivity and mental excitation, associated with prolonged fear and emotional stress and followed by exhaustion and fatigue: Thompson Indians during their spirit training were often running all night until completely fatigued. (Teit 1900) Shuswap novices leaped down mountain sides trying to keep up with rolling boulders. (Teit 1905) The Lillooet spirit seeker engaged in exhausting bodily exercises and tried to achieve a general exaltation of his senses, thereby inducing what Hill-Tout (1905a, 1905b) labelled "mystic dreams and visions in an enervated condition". The "highly sensitized mind" of a Coast Salish on spirit quest might, especially in a "weakened and feverish condition" react to any unusual occurrence in nature with semiconscious imagery (Barnett 1955), in our terminology: an altered state of consciousness. Old Pierre of Katzie in the Lower Fraser Valley was worn out and weakened from his unrelenting quest at age ten; he fell to the ground exhausted and finally had his vision. (Jenness 1955) Swinomish tutelaries often appeared to people suffering from excessive fatigue or emotional shock, or to those in severe stress situations. (Wike 1941) One young man of the Klallam obtained great power at the expense of enduring severe hardships; he lost blood, fainted, crawled home like a baby. (Gunther 1927) We may well assume that nightly vigils in a spirit-haunted wilderness aroused intense fears in most youngsters. That such emotional agitation was intended by their mentors as conducive to spirit visions can be gathered from reports of Southern Coast Salish children being sent out on their quest in stormy weather and thunderstorms. (Haeberlin 1930; Gunther 1927) They were also made to dive in presumably shark-infested waters, having to rely on sharp sticks of iron-wood for their defense. (Haeberlin 1930)

Somatopsychological factors: Under the following headings are described techniques by which altered states of consciousness were achieved in the populations under consideration here. Such manoeuvres played an important catalytic or facilitating role in the learning of "spontaneous" dissociative states. Dissociation could later be entered into without resorting to the original somatopsychic induction methods. It may be mentioned here that hallucinogenic or narcotic drugs were not used in traditional Northwest Coast cultures.

(1) Sleep deprivation: This is implied in the extended vigils of most spirit quests, but is specifically mentioned by some authors. (for example Barnett 1955, Olson 1936)

(2) Hypoglycemia due to abstention from food intake: fasting was required on all spirit quests. It was prolonged among the Interior Salish up to eight or ten days. (Teit 1900, 1905, 1930; Hill-Tout 1905a, 1905b) The Coast Salish novice, too, was expected to fast or eat very little. (Barnett 1936 and 1955) When "training" around ten or eleven years of age, Old Pierre of Katzie roamed the bush for three weeks without food intake, until aching with hunger. Nanaimo boys starved themselves to the extreme in order to induce hallucinations. (Robinson 1963) In the Southern Coast Salish area fasting would be carried on for several days among the Quinault (Olson 1936); for a week by a Swinomish seeker living on alder leaves (Wike 1941); for two weeks by another Puget Sound candidate (Haeberlin 1930); as long as a Twana youth could stand it. (Elmendorf 1960)

(3) Dehydration.

a) Dehydration due to abstention from fluid intake is specifically reported for the Thompson by Teit (1900), but was also part of the fasting regime in other Plateau groups.

b) Dehydration due to forced vomiting: Emetic, purgative and sudorific methods were employed on the quest besides bathing and cleansing in an all-out effort at purification designed to propitiate the spirits. Vomiting was induced either by mechanical means such as inserting sticks, willow or vine maple twigs, or feathers into the throat (Interior and Coast Salish groups; Teit 1900, 1905; Hill-Tout 1904, 1905a, 1905b; Jenness 1955) or by swallowing sea-water or herbal emetics. (Canadian Coast Salish; Barnett 1938, 1955).

c) Dehydration due to purgation: the young Thompson and Shuswap youths used herbal laxatives such as decoctions of the soap-berry *(Sapindus saponaria)* or berberry *(Berberis)* bush to purge themselves (Teit 1900, 1905); devil's club *(Echinopanax horridus)* was known to all Coast Salish as having laxative properties. (Jenness 1955)

d) Dehydration due to sweating: intensive sweating in sweat-lodges, often accompanied by monotonous singing and praying, was a very wide-spread ingredient of the spirit quest. (for example, Teit 1900, 1905; Hill-Tout 1904, 1905b; Duff 1952; Barnett 1955)

(4) Hypoxaemia due to hypoventilation in prolonged diving: an important procedure in Coast Salish spirit quest was diving, often to a state of exhaustion or unconsciousness in which a vision was received. (Barnett 1938) Diving in whirlpools was practised by Twana novices (Elmendorf 1960) and the Sanpoil youth was admonished to stay under water as long as possible. (Ray 1932) To obtain certain spirits a Snohomish boy had to dive into deep water carrying a heavy stone and would find himself lying on the beach when he regained consciousness (Haeberlin 1930). Nanaimo boys sometimes drowned when using the same method. (Robinson 1963)

(5) Exposure to extreme temperatures: Bathing in ice-cold water was, and still is, an even more general feature of the Salish spirit quest than the exposure to the hot temperatures of the sweathouses. At a very tender age, Old Pierre of Katzie bathed in icy pools all winter. (Jenness 1955) A Quinault informant remembered how icicles formed in his hair during such purifying baths. (Olson 1936)

(6) Self-inflicted pain stimuli: Self-tortures and scarifications, although not as prominent as on the plains, are recorded as belonging to the spirit quest of several Salish groups. There is a wide range from flagellation with nettles (Teit 1900) to cutting the finger-tips, piercing the legs, slashing the chest (Teit 1905), or lacing the body with knives. (Hill-Tout 1904) The psycho-physiological effect of self-inflicted pain is referred to by Barnett (1955) who writes of Coast Salish boys that they sometimes scarified their legs until feeling "light-footed and exhilarated".

Spirit Illness

We now have to consider references to a condition which is recorded for the entire spirit dance area, usually under the name of *spirit-* or *power illness*. This condition is in many respects analogous to Eliade's (1964) *initiatory sickness* associated with the "ecstatic initiation" of shamans. The phenomenology of initiatory sickness has been discussed elsewhere, using the example of ritualized inaugural procedures of healers in non-Western societies, and their Western equivalents; and the condition has been defined as a ritualized pathomorphic, i.e., illness-like, but not pathological state. (Jilek 1971) The relevance of this definition for the seasonal spirit illness of the Salish Indians will be shown by ethnographic data. Spier (1930) already asserted that the illness accompanying the acquisition of power among the Klamath had a parallel in the Yurok shaman novice's "pain sickness", and Barnett (1955) compared the Yurok "doctor-making" dance with Salish winter dance initiations. For most of the Coast Salish region, the advent of the winter season is heralded by the sickening of those who have acquired dancing power. (Barnett 1955) They become anorectic, insomnic, distraught, weak and emaciated. According to Ray (1939) the incidence of "personal guardian spirit illness" among the Plateau groups of the Columbia River System indicates upriver influences from the Coast; in the Interior Salish region the condition is known only to the Wenatchi, Okanagan, and Sanpoil. The return of the personal tutelary at maturity is marked by "physical disturbance varying from a feeling of lonesomeness to a severe illness", and this affliction may recur seasonally as among the Wenatchi, or the Sanpoil whose "thinking about spirits" in winter resulted in a nostalgic despondency to be alleviated only by singing and dancing. When first appearing to a person, spirit sickness took on a more severe form with localized pains, and required the shaman's assistance: the spirit was removed, the new song was revealed to the patient through the mediating therapist, and the spirit then "blown" back to the novice, whereupon the latter gave an inaugural dance. Uninitiated participants occasionally became ill at dances and were diagnosed by the shaman as suffering from guardian spirit visitation. (Ray 1932) In the southern Coast Salish province, the Twana (Elmendorf 1960) distinguished several guardian spirit-

40

connected diseases, of which the "winter illness" was the spirit illness in the restricted sense of the term used here. The shaman's diagnosis was "you are being looked at by a vision-acquired spirit", or "being made sick by your power". For the cure of winter illness, several therapeutic measures were prescribed. The patient had to sponsor a spirit dance with participation of invited guests; the therapist had to summon the guardian spirit who then possessed the patient, singing its song "from inside", and making him dance. The patient now demonstrated his spirit powers by singing, dancing, and ritual acts. Subsequent winter illnesses were diagnosed by the patient himself and required public exhibition of the spirit power by its owner in the dance ceremonial. In the Puget Sound area, Haeberlin (1930) found that a clear distinction was made between "physical illness" and the obligatory seasonal illness caused by the return of the *skalaletut* spirits at winter dance time in November. It was not necessary to consult a shaman as the patient was not considered to be "really ill"; he treated himself by singing his song and performing his dance. Among the Puyallup-Nisqually, disease due to the desire of a spirit power to demonstrate itself, was diagnosed by shamans but curable by the patient; the power could be that of the patient or that of a deceased relative. Weakness or ailment was the first sign of possession by "ceremonial power" which was to be displayed in the "power—or spirit-*sing*". (Smith 1940) Wike (1941) relates the case of an 18 year old Swinomish girl whose depressive mourning reaction with severe anxiety and conversion symptoms was not recognized by the U.S. Indian Health Service physician, but was diagnosed and "doctored" by her father, a shaman, as "power illness". The patient was cured by overcoming her acculturative resistance and finally manifesting her "warrior power" in spirit singing. She chose to become a "fine girl in the Old Indian Way", for which she was praised by the ancestors appearing in a dream. The alternative to becoming a spirit singer, she knew, would have been death. Descriptive expressions such as "that sick man", "he is like crazy", or "I've been sick so many times with that tune", are used by the Swinomish when speaking of spirit illness. (Wike 1941) As a rule, the older singers assist the novice without shamanic aid; they determine the nature of the spirit power by the new dancer's "sighs". Similarly, the Klallam of the Olympic Peninsula, when falling ill in winter through visits of their

41

guardian spirits, do not call the shaman but invite their friends to help them sing and restore health by satisfying the spirits. (Gunther 1927) "Power illness", relieved by publicly singing the songs received from potent spirits, was also identified by the Quinault. (Olson 1936) In the 1950s, the Lummi Indians would still attribute chronic illness during winter time to possession by a spirit demanding the patient to sing its song as a new dancer; all owners of spirit songs were assumed to become possessed in winter and to suffer an illness treatable only by singing and dancing. (Suttles 1954) We find analogous concepts of spirit illness in the Canadian sector of the Coast Salish province. In Curtis' time, (1913:103) spirit illness among the Cowichan (Vancouver Island) always followed a previous vision experience:

> The recollection of a vision remains constantly in the mind, and after an indefinite length of time it becomes oppressive. The breath comes with great difficulty. It is then necessary for the parents of the sufferer to invite the people to their house for a dance, and if this were not done he would become really ill and would die.

Robinson (1963) enumerates symptoms of "power sickness" among the Nanaimo of Vancouver Island, caused by siəwən—possession: restlessness, fainting spells, uncontrollable crying, heavy breathing, sighing and moaning. Lodging in the owner's chest, the power ascends to the throat in the beginning of the winter season, to "burst forth as sound, simultaneously taking possession of its owner and turning him into a manifestation of the power itself". The shaman's help is then sought to "bring out" the dance song through initiation procedures, or to "bury" the song temporarily in the patient's back until such time as initiation to spirit dancing might more conveniently be arranged. For some years the newly initiated dancer can expect difficulties in controlling his siəwən which may be aroused suddenly and again cause power illness if not quickly pacified by singing and dancing. The line of demarcation between conscious and unconscious motivation is quite thin, as evidenced by Robinson's (1963:139) reference to the young girls who make an effort to obtain initiation prematurely. Seasonal lassitude, lack of appetite, chest pains, crying spells and "singing" during sleep are taken as symptoms of spirit illness by the neighbouring Cowichan Indians. (Lane 1953) As with the Nanaimo, the shaman confirms the cause of the malaise and either prepares the afflicted for spirit dancing or "hides" the power in the patient's back, thereby only delaying spirit dance induction which eventually has to take place if the relapse into spirit sickness with its culturally expected lethal outcome is to be prevented. Sometimes a diagnostic error may occur and lead to the induction of a person without spirit power, suffering from some "ordinary sickness". To the Musqueam near Vancouver, B.C. (Kew 1970), *syə'wən* power has the nature of a force in itself, very much like a contagious illness, curable only by "bringing out the *syə'wən*" in proper singing and dancing. "Getting the *syə'wən* straight" by correct costume, song and dance, removes the symptoms of spirit illness which include feelings of weakness, unrest, spastic pains in thorax and back, even unconsciousness, and which may lead to death if manifestation of the power is not achieved. This is reported to have happened to an Upper Stalo woman who was in the city when surprised by her song; "she fought it off and they brought her home in a coffin". (Duff 1952:107) Fainting as a cardinal symptom of seasonal spirit illness was mentioned by other Upper Stalo informants. (Duff 1952) Power-sickness was given as the major reason for spirit dance initiation in Musqueam, and is seen as coming each fall down the Fraser River to Chilliwack, then turning southward to Lummi, from there to Musqueam and finally crossing over to Vancouver Island. (Kew 1970) The power "seems to come from the East" as one of Duff's (1952) informants put it; it is perceived as spreading down the Fraser Valley to the Pacific Coast and to the Island like a seasonal epidemic. The Katzie of the Lower Fraser Valley (Jenness 1955) amalgamated the concept of spirit illness with that of "vitality-loss" manifested by depressive brooding, self-isolation, general debility; and attributed to the vitality leaving the patient's body and lingering at the guardian spirit's home. Shamanic dream analysis provided the diagnostic clues, and facial painting in accordance with the specific spirit dance pattern lured the vitality back. The patient, who immediately intoned the power-song given to him by the guardian spirit, was initiated as a dancer, whereupon the spirit restored his health. Old Pierre the famous Katzie medicine-man, was able to make the differential diagnosis between "real

43

sickness" and *sia'wən*—sickness:

> Jack is not really ill. He has only lost his vitality. Some guardian spirit has it. He needs . . . an old dancer who has a powerful guardian spirit, to restore him to health.
>
> When we came to where Gus was lying, my uncle said: 'You had better chant one of your medicine songs and summon your medicine-power.' I felt Gus' stomach, however, and replied: 'No, I shall not chant for my medicine spirit, but for my dance spirit.'

Old Pierre confirmed that spirit illness was fatal if not diagnosed and managed appropriately: "In recent years . . . several Indians have died, or nearly died, because their songs became confused and could not issue." (Jenness 1955:41, 48, 43) Of great interest is the history of a superficially acculturated Katzie woman raised in a Catholic convent and married to a white American, mother of highly educated children. This lady suffered from what appears to have been a post-menopausal depression with somatic complaints, unsuccessfully treated and presumably misdiagnosed by medical specialists, but revealed to the discerning mind of Old Pierre as caused by cultural estrangement. Health was restored with Old Pierre's assistance when the patient exhibited the Thunder Spirit already possessed by her (unacculturated) uncle. (Jenness 1955:59)

Spirit Dance Initiation

If guardian spirit possession is, as we have seen, conceived of as causing an illness curable only by spirit dancing, then Suttles (1963:519) is right in stating that "the initiation of a new dancer is a form of shamanistic treatment." Robinson (1963) speaks of the initiates as of "patients", "treated" by old dancers some of whom are shamans. The initiation of a new spirit dancer is also, as Kew (1970) has termed it, a "classic *rite de passage* which marks a change in life status." To many contemporary Salish Indians it is still equivalent to death and rebirth. The neophyte does in reality pass through an altered state of consciousness and in the

44

process he often actually suffers a temporary loss of consciousness[4] as we ourselves observed during initiation ceremonies at local winter dances in the Upper Stalo region. In this context it should be remembered that both John Slocum, the (Salish) founder of the Shaker cult, and Smohalla, the (Sahaptin) prophet of the "Dreamer" religion, which was an immediate precursor of the Ghost Dance, where legitimized in their mission by death and resurrection, i.e., by losing and regaining consciousness—the one in an accident, the other in combat. (cf. Mooney 1896; Barnett 1957)

Loss of consciousness during spirit dance initiation rituals is frequently reported in the ethnographic literature on Salish cultures. The initiate was "by any means possible rendered unconscious", he was "beaten, smothered and choked until he was unconscious" and said to be "paralyzed, dead". (Barnett 1955:278; 1938:137) Some 60 years ago, Curtis (1913:104) was told of the winter dance initiation procedure of the Cowichan on Vancouver Island:

> A number of men; usually five; who at some previous time have passed through what the young man is now to experience, dance backward in a line, and then forward toward the young man, each one blowing into his face as they approach him, and making motions at his face with sticks. After a while he becomes unconscious and rigid. The dance ceases, and the parents put the young man to bed, where he remains as long as three or four days, still unconscious.

Unconsciousness or fainting of spirit dance novices is also mentioned by Duff (1952), Hill-Tout (1900), Jenness (1955), Lane (1953), Robinson (1963), Stern (1934) and Wike (1941).

As before in the case of the guardian spirit vision-quest, we now have to consider the forces at work in the production of altered states of consciousness during spirit dance initiations. Above all, we must not overlook one force never mentioned but ever-present at the ceremonials, namely that of culturally conditioned collective suggestion. The meaning of culturally conditioned collective suggestion in the context of therapy is best characterized by quoting Leighton (1968:1177):

45

Every individual is prepared during the course of his life by a set of expectancies regarding illness and treatment which are part of his culture. These are inculcated long before his own condition as a patient comes about. They are heightened, however, as he approaches being a patient and increase the suggestive power of many of the experiences he undergoes.

Collective suggestion is built into any effective psychotherapy anywhere as an important prerequisite for the success of individual treatment procedures which are largely specific to culture area, historical period, and prevailing ideology: an agnostic rationalist is not likely to be cured when shipped to Lourdes, nor a Pavlovian when placed on a psychoanalyst's couch. By the same token, the local Salish Indians would not expect urban middle-class Whites to catch spirit illness and to be genuinely possessed even after repeated exposure to the spectacle of spirit dancing. However, to the average young Indian person of the Upper Stalo region it is still reality that old dancers and Indian Doctors can make him dance and sing whether he wants it or not, for their paraphernalia hold dancer's power and if they hit him with the cane or rattle he will faint or "die" to be resurrected as a dancer; the ritual "workers" never fail to produce the intended effect. (cf. Duff 1952; Jenness 1955) This omnipresent collective suggestion is the background against which the conditions operant in the production of altered states of consciousness in spirit dance initiates have to be seen.

The following list categorizes ethnographic observations on the basis of neuropsychological findings. (cf. Ludwig 1968) It includes conditions of increased external stimulation and motor hyperactivity, alternating with those of reduced external stimulation and motor hypoactivity, both associated with somato-psychological factors.

(1) *Psychic shock:* "grabbing" or "clubbing", the first act of initiation, consists of a surprise attack on the prospective new dancer. He is, at least in theory, not apprized of his fate, but at an unexpected moment seized by husky ritualist-aides with blackened faces who rush at him and lift him up helplessly, whereupon he expects to be "clubbed" with the power-filled cane or rattle of the officiating ritualist or Indian Doctor, possibly to

be manhandled, or even thrown into ice-cold water. (cf. Barnett 1938, 1955; Duff 1952; Kew 1970; Lane 1953; Stern 1934)

(2) *Seclusion and restricted mobility:* the initiation period proper lasts four to five days in the Canadian Coast Salish area (cf. Barnett 1938, 1955; Duff 1952; Jenness 1955; Kew 1970; Lane 1953; Robinson 1963), up to 8 days in some Puget Sound groups. (Wike 1941) During much of this time the initiate is secluded in a compartment or cubicle, guarded by his attendants and kept inactive; except for bouts of physical exertion he has to lie still and avoid body movements. (Barnett 1955; Lane 1953)

(3) *Forced hypermotility:* the initiate is sent on a "run" to disappear into the woods[5] accompanied by attendant(s). He trots through the bush for hours until exhausted and "half-crazed". (Jenness 1955) This "run" may last for the whole day and include swimming and diving (Barnett 1955), it may be repeated on four consecutive mornings as among the Swinomish (Wike 1941); in modern times it may be substituted by a chase round the longhouse. (Kew 1970) During the "run" the neophyte may obtain his new song. (Duff 1952)

(4) *Visual-sensory deprivation:* the novice is blindfolded with a dark kerchief (Kew 1970), a protective device against the harmful glances of menstruating women. (Lane 1953) In his cubicle he is also totally covered with blankets. (Barnett 1955; Kew 1970)

(5) *Sleep deprivation:* the candidate sleeps very little for several days during the initiation period. (Haeberline 1930)

(6) *Kinetic stimulation:* the "grabbed" initiate is held horizontally at chest height by the helpers, often thrown up in the air, and hurriedly carried around. (cf. Barnett 1955; Jenness 1955; Kew 1970; Lane 1953)

(7) *Acoustic stimulation:* the initiating "workers" chant and pray loudly (Jenness 1955), make stereotyped sounds, sing their songs for hours (Kew 1970) or even days (Barnett 1955), continuously shaking their deer hoof rattles or beating their sticks. (cf. Barnett 1955; Jenness 1955; Kew 1970; Wike 1941) The monotonous beating of cedar boards at Squamish dances sent the dancers into "hypnotic trances". (Hill-Tout 1900)

Rhythmic drumming is of paramount importance in Coast Salish winter ceremonials, and the loud beating of rapid rhythms on dozens of deer-hide drums, some quite close to the novice, is a characteristic feature of spirit dance initiations. (cf. Barnett 1938,

1955; Duff 1952; Jenness 1955; Kew 1970; Wike 1941)

(8) *Algetic stimulation:* The novice is beaten (Barnett 1938, 1955), hit with the ceremonial deer hoof cane or rattle on stomach or head (Duff 1952); he is bitten on the exposed chest and abdomen (Kew 1970), or even poked there with hot staffs to force out his song. (Lane 1953)

(9) *Temperature stimulation:* (a) Cold: New dancers are made to bathe in wintry rivers, pools, or in the sea every morning. (cf. Jenness 1955; Kew 1970; Wike 1941) During the initiation ceremony they are unexpectedly showered with cold water and this hydrotherapeutic shock drives them into a frenzy (Jenness 1955) and brings out the anticipated involuntary cry. (Kew 1970) (b) Heat: the novice has to lie covered with blankets from head to feet, he is "roasted" and "overheated". (Barnett 1955:278)

(10) *Asphyxiation:* the candidate is subjected to suffocating treatment; he may be held under water, or several old dancers may exhale their breath, i.e. their power, into his mouth (Barnett 1955); until he "blackens out" and then experiences a vision—a "fool-proof" but expensive method to obtain spirit power among the Nanaimo. (Robinson 1963:123) However, the blowing of power in to the novice in spirit dance initiation is foremost an act of symbolic significance and does not, as a rule, involve the breathing of exhaled air.

(11) *Dehydration:* throughout the initiation period, i.e. for at least four to five days, neophytes are allowed to drink only a minimum. (cf. Barnett 1955; Duff 1952; Jenness 1955; Kew 1970; Wike 1941). They have to suck water through bone tubes or hollow branches—today also through glass or plastic tubes tied around their neck—while at the same time perspiring heavily when dancing or running. A Sanpoil initiate was not permitted to take any fluid at all during the four-night period of his inaugural dance. (Ray 1932)

(12) *Hypoglycemia* due to fasting: total abstention from food intake for four to five days is customary in many Salish spirit dance initiations. (cf. Barnett 1955; Haeberlin 1930; Jenness 1955; Kew 1970; Ray 1932; Wike 1941) The neophytes' subjection to this strict fasting is Hill-Tout's (1900) explanation for the ease with which they pass into "hypnotic" states. The regime of mortification is rendered more difficult to tolerate by manoeuvres and prescriptions which have a frustrating effect on

48

the initiate: bits of food, when finally placed in his mouth after repeated faints, have to be spit out (Jenness 1955; Kew 1970); water is handed to him in leaking containers and taken away again before he can quench his thirst. (Duff 1952)

Footnotes

1. Cf. Rodewyk's (1963) recent "differential diagnosis" between religious experiences, hysterical states, and daemoniac possessions.

2. "Cette théatralité de l'existence hysterique ou le nevrosé joue son rôle comme un acteur." (Ey 1963:405)

3. In the present monograph, the term *syə'wən* (or *syə́wən*, as some linguists prefer), following contemporary usage in the mainland Coast Salish area, denotes the spiritual powers acquired by individuals in a prescribed way, and manifested in the spirit ceremonial through specific song, dance, face painting, and other attributes displayed during the so-called *syə'wən* season. In this sense, and in contemporary usage, *syə'wən* refers to the spiritual essence of the whole ceremonial and comprises more than the individual dancer's song.

4. The kind of "little death", a collapse phenomenon seen by the neuro-psychiatrist Sargant (1967) during initiatory procedures in Africa, which reminded him of abreactive techniques in psychiatry.

5. Cf., C.G. Jung's comment on this archetype: "Das Verschwinden und Verstecken im Wald . . . deutet auf Tod und Wiedergeburt." ("Disappearing and hiding in the woods . . . points to death and rebirth", Jung 1952:411)

Chapter Four

Contemporary Spirit Illness and Anomic Depression

Note on Anomie and Relative Deprivation

The concept of anomie, introduced in 1897 by Durkheim in its original form, has found a classical interpretation by Talcott Parsons:

> Not merely contractual relations, but stable social relations in general, and even the *personal equilibrium* of the members of a social group are seen to be dependent on the existence of a normative structure in relation to conduct, generally accepted as having moral authority by the members of the community, and upon their effective subordination to these norms ... When this controlling normative structure is upset and disorganized, individual conduct is equally disorganized and chaotic ... *Anomie* is precisely this state of disorganization where the hold of norms over individual conduct has broken down. (Parsons 1949:377)

> The polar antithesis of full institutionalization is, however, *anomie* ... the complete breakdown of normative order in both senses. (Parsons 1951:39)

Durkheim's concept of anomie as *absence of societal norms* was widened by Merton (1938) to include a pre-stage: the lack of coordination of the means—and—goals phases of the social structure, finally leading to "cultural chaos or anomie". He viewed such a "dissociation between culturally defined aspirations and socially structured means" as generating both social and psychic pathology. It is hardly coincidental that analogous conclusions were drawn in the field of psychopathology by Horney (1937). Both the sociologist and the psychiatrist made their observations in North America where, as Merton (1938:680) put it:

...the channels of vertical mobility are closed or narrowed *in a society which places a high premium on economic affluence and social ascent for all its members* ... The same body of success-symbols is held to be desirable for all. These goals are held to *transcend class lines*, not to be bounded by them, yet the actual social organization is such that there exist class differentials in the accessibility of these *common* success-symbols. Frustration and thwarted aspiration lead to the search for avenues of escape from a culturally induced intolerable situation; or unrelieved ambition may eventuate in illicit attempts to acquire the dominant values. The American stress on pecuniary success and ambitiousness for all thus invites exaggerated anxieties, hostilities, neuroses and antisocial behaviour.

It appears permissible to conclude on the basis of Merton's formulations, that individuals who realize that the goal of material success and affluence, widely advertised and emphasized as universally attainable in the society they live in, is actually beyond their reach by the means sanctioned in this very society, suffer from what Aberle (1966:322-329) has termed *relative deprivation:* "a negative discrepancy between legitimate expectation and actuality, or between legitimate expectation and anticipated actuality, or both." If the members of a culturally or racially defined minority group within the larger society, are encouraged to legitimately expect a "Just Society" with equally good opportunities for everybody regardless of racial or cultural properties, but in actuality perceive themselves as disadvantaged because of these properties, then this whole group will suffer from *relative deprivation*, which, as Aberle points out, is "measured by a comparison of the actual or expected condition of an individual or a group with his, or its, legitimate expectations." Aberle stresses that relative deprivation is a "social and cultural phenomenon". However, insofar as individuals react to this phenomenon, it has important psychological correlates just as Durkheim's absence of a normative structure and Merton's means-goals disjunction have.

In over ten years of psychiatric epidemiological investigation in the Stirling County Study, the Leightons (1963) and their multidisciplinary team have found a significant association of psychiatric symptom formation with *sociocultural disin-*

tegration.[1] Of relevance to our discussion is that the research findings suggested to them a prominent role of the following mechanisms by which sociocultural disintegration fosters psychopathology:

a) "by interfering with the achievement of socially valued ends by legitimate means";
b) "by interfering with the individual's sense of membership in a moral order";

also, although less pronounced:

c) "by interfering with a person's orientation regarding his place in society"; and
d) "by interfering with a person's membership in a definite human group".

Among the indicators of sociocultural disorganization found to be of relevance to the established higher prevalence of psychiatric disorder in disintegrated communities, were secularization and cultural confusion, which both refer to Durkheim's concept of anomie. *Cultural confusion* was defined as "weakening of norms derived from membership in a particular cultural group when the members of this group are brought into close contact with the contrasting norms of a different cultural group and are unable to integrate the two sets." (*op. cit.*:387) Here we should be reminded that "contacts between groups of radically different culture often involve deprivation for some or many members of one of these groups." (Aberle 1966:326)

Anomic Depression as Important Background Phenomenon of Contemporary Spirit Illness

In this section we shall try to demonstrate how, in the population under discussion, experiences of cultural confusion and relative deprivation precipitate the psychic state we propose to call *anomic depression*. Anomic depression is a chronic dysphoric state characterized by feelings of existential frustration, discouragement, defeat, lowered self-esteem and sometimes moral disorientation. This state is often the basis of the specific psychic and psychophysiologic symptom-formation manifested by contemporary sufferers from spirit illness who turn to spirit dancing for genuinely therapeutic reasons.

52

The reader familiar with ethnographic literature will wonder why anomic depression should be given such a prominent place in a discussion of Coast Salish spirit illness. It would indeed be difficult to find in the older ethnographic reports anything like spirit illness with depressive symptoms *in the context of cultural and social deprivation.* To be sure, the signs of spirit illness were always expressive of distress and suffering. Nevertheless, it was the essence of traditional spirit illness that such sufferings were actually a reward, anticipated by those who had previously sought spirit power individually; and the so-called illness was not more than the strictly seasonal, highly stereotyped pathomorphic prelude to the public exhibition of this power in the dance ceremonial. This is the impression conveyed to us by the earlier ethnographers. However, in more recent reports we occasionally read case descriptions which would fit into our category of *anomic depression.* There is, for example Wike's (1941, *vide supra*) story of the depressed girl who, through spirit singing, found back to the "Old Indian Way"; or the cure through spirit dancing of the melancholic lady who had become estranged from her Indian culture, related by Jenness (1955, *vide supra*). This is the type of case history which we often encountered in our own investigations in the Upper Stalo region and which caused us to consult the literature on the anomie—question and to formulate our concept of anomic depression:

The following samples of Indian statements will illustrate the character of anomic depression.

The non-Indian might have pain, but there generally seems to be a time when it lets up. But in our people, it's been a continuous pain, it's a continuous painful existence for the Indian . . . many of them say I don't belong anywhere, where am I going, what is my purpose? I'm existing, that's all. I suffered it myself, it's right in the stomach, it's plain confusion . . . It is painful to not feel worth and belonging, the Indian person grows up most of his life with nothing, but he sees the White men around him have so much that he would like to have. After a while the Indians quit wanting anything, they give up hope. . . to want is wrong, so they use alcohol, but it's depression . . . (L.S.)

53

The main reason for depression among Indians is loneliness, no more togetherness, and bitterness that they took
away our land and our culture . . . The people should have a
better life for what they have had to sacrifice in this
country, this is one of the biggest reasons of why people are
so bitter . . . Most young people have no idea of their background and language, they go home to their little old shacks
and half the time they're intoxicated, so they lose all their
pride . . . My sons have always complained to me that they
are the under-dogs, no matter where they go they feel they
are discriminated, the only way they can be happy is in an
Indian life [i.e., spirit dancing] . . . I guess they [new
dancers] were depressed because they were bored by the
sort of life they had. (Y.I.)

If I had kept up with my Indian ways I could have accepted things better than I do now . . . I can't seem to
accept myself . . . I myself as a child looked down on anything like the Indian way, it came from the teaching that
was put into me . . . it really began when I was working out
and the people looked down at me because I was an Indian
. . . but I kept on being my quiet little self not showing
anything almost as if I was saying please be nice to me . . . I
have had so much hate in me, after a while I do not even
know what the hate is about . . . It was against the Church
to believe in the Indian and to do these things [spirit
dancing] . . . I went to the priest yesterday, and felt good,
but after a little while I was so sick again. (N.B.)

I got integrated into white society, away from the reserve.
I was put in a place that I really wanted, but in order to get
it I had to leave my people. I can't go back to my people's
place, they call me down, but I don't think I am better than
they are . . . I think I want to be an Indian dancer because I
am so lonely . . . I often dream I am getting clubbed I can't
sleep and I sweat, I get up 3 or 4 o'clock in the morning
and there is this pain in there, it makes me want to cry, I
feel it right in my stomach. This thing comes on through
the sorrow that you've built up inside you, it makes you
want to holler. If I go to be an Indian dancer, they won't

have to club me, its *šiwi'l* [supernatural power] as they call it in Indian. (D.O.)

I was Indian before I went away from home to go to residential school, and there they punished me for talking Indian. When they beat that Indian spirit out of me, my whole body went to sleep, I got paralyzed, laid helpless. One of the doctors in the medical profession took me to an Indian doctor, and by gosh, the feelings came back to my legs . . . I hated that Indian language . . . when I came back my grandmother wanted to pick up where she left off, but I got mad and said I'm a White man now, don't bother me with that Indian . . . they'd knocked that Indian out of me and put the White man's way of life there, but it didn't do me any good . . . I was already singing when I was 17, it was all there, but then I said this: nobody is going to see me jumping up and down like an old monkey [i.e., spirit dancing]—that's what I thought of my own people. But then I was sick for seven years, my face just dead color as you see a person laying in the coffin, no life in me 'cause I was not eating . . . I wanted to be a White man, was ashamed that I was Indian, I had that low down feeling in me. It took me 7 years to wake up to that I was Indian . . . all they had to do was to sing and drum for me as soon as I say I was well . . . if it wasn't that I woke up in time to the fact that I was Indian I'd be dead now, 'cause there is a time when it is too late. (Prominent ritualist)

Most of the case histories obtained on severe spirit illness reveal the following pattern, which may be called the psychodynamics of anomic depression: a) acculturation imposed through western education; b) attempt at White identification ("identification with the aggressor" in psychoanalytic terms), or vying for acceptance by Whites; c) subjective experience of rejection and discrimination—awareness of relative deprivation in White society; d) cultural identity confusion; e) moral disorientation, often with acting-out behaviour; f) guilt about denial of Indian-ness— depressive and psychophysiologic symptom formation— inefficiency of Western remedies; g) diagnosis as spirit illness permitting reidentification with aboriginal culture via initiation into spirit dancing ("death and rebirth"); h) alternatively, if initiation prevented by outside factors, ongoing symptom formation, often with intrafamily conflict.

The Symptomatology of Contemporary Spirit Illness

The symptoms of spirit illness, as elicited from our informants, resemble those of neurotic depressions in Western cultures. They include anorexia, insomnia, apathy alternating with restlessness; dysphoric moods with crying spells and nostalgic despondency, somatizations such as pain in abdomen, chest or back, sometimes also conversion reactions (psychogenic paralyses and fainting spells). When occurring during the ceremonial season, any of these symptoms may be attributed to *syə'wən* possession. There are other signs which we found to be of diagnostic significance, and these will be discussed below.

In the foreground of the syndrome and generally emphasized is the melancholia aspect of spirit illness. The depressive reaction appears often to be triggered or aggravated by mourning, or by memories of deceased ancestors and other old-timers, or of the Indian past which in retrospect appears as a Golden Age.[2] Nostalgic and melancholic ruminations of this type preoccupy the patient's mind more and more as spirit illness progresses. A few quotations from case histories suffice to demonstrate this:

When we bring back the names of our old people we start to cry . . . (Ritualist at post-initiation ceremonial)

I started going into moods of crying . . . here am I now in this world and there on that side is people that have gone a long time ago and it is so sad, and I am in between, sometimes I am here and sometimes over there. (N.B.)

I lost my first child, that's the first time I sang . . . most of the songs are sorrow . . . Some Catholic women said that *syə'wən*, that's the devil's—but when there is a death in their family and they're crying, invariably they start to sing . . . (L.S.)

Sadness and sorrow is the very beginning of *syə'wən*-illness. (E.S.)

56

You get nervous, you can no longer laugh, it's said, it's a sad thing . . . You are always afraid of something. (C.L.)

When my aunt died I was feeling so bad that I did not go to her funeral up the lake . . . my mother used to tell me 'when somebody of our people dies you got to be there and try to help', now I blame myself . . . that's when it started real bad. (D.O.)

I come here tonight with a troubled mind . . . Sleep is something I have departed from in the last weeks. I expect I will need more help than I ever wanted all my life . . . today my life is going to ruin me, I am going through hell. Why did this happen to me? Death is not far away . . . I know two people, the most happy people I know. Pow-wow, that is the life these two people lead . . . (Prospective dancer two months before initiation, addressing A.A. meeting)

Symptoms peculiar to spirit illness as manifested today, i.e. symptoms of culture-specific and pathognomonic significance, are:
a) singing and "hollering" in sleep:

I was heard to be singing in my sleep all the time . . . like these people [hospitalized Indian patients] they were hollering, as soon as they laid down to go to sleep they'd start singing. (E.S.)

She started singing in her sleep when she was 16, her father used to have to wake her up because she'd holler and cry—she dreamt about her song. (G.N.)

When I first came to the hospital, I felt like singing but I could not . . . I sang the song quietly to myself that helped me to get rid of the pain, a pressure in the chest . . . they say I sang in sleep. (R.L.)

b) hallucinatory or illusional perceptions of a psychogenic (non-schizophrenic) type and of culture-specific content; such as visions of guardian spirits, deceased dancers, ceremonial paraphernalia and acts; hearing of spirit songs:

What's known as Sasquatch, I'd seen him around all the

57

time, he was talking English to me . . . I wouldn't tell anybody, they'd think I am losing my mind. (E.S.)

When I was out hunting and I saw the deer it seemed to change, it seemed to watch me and it was like winter dance spirit . . . I got scared . . . I hear that song when I listen to the wind and to the waterfall. Once I went right underneath the waterfall and I cried, I wanted to be relieved by dancing. (D.O.)

I started hearing this Indian song in jail, so I sang it too. It was a very sad song, I cried . . . I could hear them in the hospital, too, all old songs and they were all so sad . . . the pipes from the laundry, they were making a noise, all day and all night on, songs going through my head because of it. I feel so bad when I hear the song, but when I sing it I feel better . . . sometimes I see food coming towards my mouth, it is so real that I open my mouth to bite [i.e., as if fed during initiation] it means something the Indian way, a bad sign of serious illness. (N.B.)

c) Another quite typical finding is that of dyspnea with sighing respiration. This has also been described in some severe depressions of Europeans and White Americans (cf. Burns 1971; Ayd 1961). Its frequent occurrence in contemporary spirit illness underlines the depression-like character of this condition. A culture-specifc explanation for this symptom is the supernaturally caused lack of air around the patient afflicted by spirit illness:

Mostly there's no air. I'd catch myself gasping, trying to absorb more air, I would light a match and it would go out for lack of oxygen . . . there just wasn't any air. (Prominent ritualist)

This type of dyspnea is quite dramatic and often arouses the concern of those who observe it. One young Indian defendant and prospective spirit dancer started to "sigh" during a court procedure (Chilliwack 1971) and asked to be remanded on account of sickness—his request was granted. In one of the patients with spirit illness, admitted to Chilliwack General Hospital, respiratory distress was so prominent that cardiac disease and congestive failure had been suspected, but was ruled out.

Today, the diagnosis of spirit illness is largely made *per exclusionem:* if physician and laboratory fail to elicit an underlying organic disorder, but also if medical attention affords no relief, the above-mentioned syndrome will be classified as *"Indian sickness"* or *"syǝ'wǝn sickness"*. In other words, differential diagnosis between "ordinary illness" and spirit sickness is mainly based on negative physical findings, as is the "diagnosis" of psychiatric disorder by poor clinicians in Western medicine. This is recognized as a deficiency in diagnostic acumen by the ritualists themselves:

> The old-timers used to know when a person has got Indian sickness but us guys, we go by the medical doctor unless we hear them holler—then we know he's got it. The only other way we know nowadays is when a medical doctor can't find nothing wrong with him. (L.O.)

Perhaps the most terse of modern definitions of spirit illness was given us by R.E.:

> What White doctors cannot cure and don't recognize, just give you b.s. talk or some aspirin for, that is very often spirit sickness. Only Indians get it, only Indian Doctors recognize it, but often the people themselves already know it.

True spirit sickness calls for initiation into spirit dancing. However, if there are valid reasons for postponing this necessary step, the Indian Doctor or ritualist can "work" on the afflicted to "set the power back", albeit not for a long time and not repeatedly. (E.S.,A.M., L.S.) Spirit illness may also be alleviated temporarily by leaving one's song in trust with an older family member. (D.O.) But any attempt to take away the power in order to prevent the afflicted from spirit dancing is made at the peril of the patient's life, as the following story of an instant initiation tells:

> Dad brought her into the big smokehouse to Doctor Mac,

who was a real strong Indian Doctor in Chehalis. Dad offered to pay $200 to take that Indian Power away from her, he didn't want her to become a dancer. Doctor Mac sat her down, put a blanket over her head, then took the blanket away and took her power out—and she dropped, she just died right there, lay there stiff, really dead. Doctor Mac told my Dad 'That's the way she'll be all the time if you take that power out'. Dad said 'put it back there!'. So Doctor Mac got a feather, stuck it in her hair, and she just started to holler and sing; she rose and started to dance, and they put the uniform on her and the hat.[3] (D.O.)

Spirit illness can be contracted through close contact with a powerful spirit dancer. This was to play a major role in the revival of spirit dancing in the Upper Stalo region: the first new dancer to be initiated here is said to have fallen ill while assisting Chief Malloway. The young man's parents were taken by surprise, and later elaborated on these events in an interview with Mr. Lloyd Mackay of the local newspaper:

> Mr. Point indicated that two of their sons have already been initiated preparatory to being spirit dancers. He and his wife related the unusual experience involving the initiation of son Jeff. Jeff had been suffering acute depressions and would sometimes go into convulsions, said Mrs. Point. In addition he would sometimes break into a strange song. Doctors could find nothing wrong and they consulted with Chief Richard Malloway who suggested that the young man was trying to relate to his spirit. The Points took Jeff to Musqueam reserve near Vancouver where there is a longhouse. He entered the initiation procedure and when it was complete 'he was completely there'. (The Chilliwack Progress, July 8, 1970:3B)

In general, spirit power is considered to be potentially contagious. Spirit sickness has been caught by laymen who *volunteered* to assist the workers in lifting up the novice during the initiation procedure (L.O.), or who "inadvertently" touched a dancer's "stick",[4] headdress or other paraphernalia charged with spirit power.

60

Sensitive persons have shown symptoms of *syə'wən* possession when just attending a "pow-wow" (R.L.) where "all sorts of power is floating around" (R.U.), or even when only listening to old Indian songs at a social gathering in winter time (D.O.). We saw one Indian patient with acute anxiety and strange body sensations triggered by sitting on a new dancer's blanket at a ceremonial. (N.L.) There is also the belief that spirit illness may be actively transferred by dancers who point their finger and "shoot spiritually" at vulnerable spectators:

> They've done that to my son, he was watching the dances, and he felt it right in the side, somebody pointed at him ... now he goes into tantrums like if you should become a singer. (R.T.)

We conclude this chapter by making the following points to clarify the concept of *anomic depression:*

1) The label anomic depression is introduced here not to suggest the existence of a new clinical entity, but to denote a psychic, psycho-physiologic and behavioural syndrome encountered in the population under discussion; a syndrome which essentially corresponds to *spirit illness* as presenting today in the Upper Stalo area.

2) The term depression is used to denote a cluster of symptoms similar to that labelled neurotic or reactive depression[5] in the language of modern Western psychiatry. Our data on symptom formation and behaviour prior to spirit dance initiation (*vide infra*, 83) suggest that candidates with predominantly depressive-psychophysiologic and with predominantly aggressive-antisocial manifestations are approximately equally represented. However, in either of these two groups we find cases with both depressive and aggressive reactions, albeit with one of these two responses in the foreground of the picture. In establishing indications for spirit dance therapy, senior ritualists tend to consider both depressive and aggressive behaviour to be in the same category (*vide infra*, 80). In the context of anomic depression, these modes of behaviour may be conceived of as intrapunitive and extrapunitive reactions.

3) The term anomic denotes that the psychodynamics involved reflect the prominent influence of those social and cultural

processes which were sketched in the note preceding this chapter. The syndrome of anomic depression is seen as a specific pattern of individual reactions to systemic and inter-systemic events.

4) Clinical experience and research data convey the impression that in the Upper Stalo population the symptom formation denoted by the term anomic depression, is closely related to the individual's subjective experience of what was defined above as anomie, relative deprivation, and cultural confusion. Sample quotations (53-58) illustrate how these socio-cultural phenomena are experienced by Coast Salish Indians.

5) Credit for having discovered the relevance of these socio-cultural phenomena to the syndrome of anomic depression among Coast Salish Indians is not due to this author, but to the Salish ritualists of our day who recognize the need for a culture-congenial therapy—the revived spirit dance ceremonial—to combat the pathogenic effects of cultural confusion, anomie, and relative deprivation among their people.

Footnotes

1. For the indicator-definitions of sociocultural disintegration see Leighton et al. (1963:369-389).

2. For example, "The Indian used to be a different kind of a person, he lived in a Garden of Eden here . . . " (Y.I.)

3. New dancers of both sexes wear a long woollen headdress covering head, face and shoulders, during the season of their initiation. They hold on to a long pointed "pole" adorned with scarfs, feathers and deer hoofs, which is discarded at the end of the season, hidden away in the forest. The novices' outfit has changed very little from that shown on an old photograph published by Barnett (1955: plate xxviii). The garb of the fully established Coast Salish spirit dancer is also still essentially the traditional costume depicted on Curtis' (1913:74) photograph, with the human hair and feather head-dress of a "black face" dancer. An innovation in the novice's

uniform are colorful headdress-ribbons with the date and place of his rebirth, for example, "T. of Chehalis taken at LaConner Feb. 5, 1970". Spirit dancers do not wear their uniform on non-ceremonial occasions, except for off season public performances of Indian dances such as during Cultus Lake Indian Festival which takes place every June near Chilliwack.

4. $k^w\partial cmi'n^?$ (Halkomelem), ceremonial staff with supernatural properties, may call its owner home in an emergency. (C.L.) Usually a carved staff decorated with individual designs, on top a human or animal head and deer hoof pendants.

5. No clear distinction can be made between reactive and neurotic depression; (cf. Bleuler 1960:461), who uses the pertinent term "psychoreactive disturbances" to distinguish conditions of a reactive and neurotic type from cerebro-organic, somato-psychic, and "endogenous" disorders.

Chapter Five

The Therapeutic Process of Contemporary Spirit Dance Initiation

Death and Rebirth—The Therapeutic Myth

The death-and-rebirth myth is the central theme of the collective suggestions surrounding the spirit dance initiation. In the view of contemporary Salish ritualists[1], the gift of obtaining power, and of healing through power, was universal to all Indians in the distant past as part of their "Indian ways", but has been lost by most of them today as a result of their emulation of the White man, who, by definition, lacks this "Indian power". The genuine shamanic healing power was a divine compensation for the technological assets of White civilization:

> The Indian was so strong in the old days, just about every old man and every old woman was an Indian Doctor in them days; they were a powerful people. God did not overlook the Indians because he gave them a few words and he blessed their hands whereby they can overcome sickness with words and if not, they can take it away. This was the power the Indian had. (E.S.)

In times still remembered by the oldtimers, shamanic power was concentrated in the Indian Doctors whose feats are still recounted to the young initiates as part of *syə'wən* lore. The senior ritualists prefer to be called "Indian leaders" or "elders". They are looked upon by other Indians as "leaders that are doing treatments" (Y.I.). If questioned, people will state that "true Indian Doctors" are no longer active in the Coast Salish area, with the possible exception of Mr. Isadore Tom of Lummi. However, among the local Indian population, ritualists are widely referred to as Indian Doctors, or are at least assumed to possess "doctoring power" to an extent that it would be presumptuous to compete with them, for example, at the *lahal* game:

> They have a powerful mind, it's no use playing when them

Indian Doctors are there . . . they just look at you and read what side you got it on right now and that's it . . . that's not just guessing, this is knowing, you see, you can't fool them. (L.T.)

In contemporary *syə'wən* theory, as taught by the ritualists, it is *syə'wən* which acts through the initiator on the initiate, and it is *syə'wən*, not the initiator, which cures the novice, burying his ailments and conflicts together with his old personality and at the same time giving him rebirth into a new life:

We came to help put him into *syə'wən*, to take his life, make a better life for himself. So you see my dear ones that's what this can do to a man or woman when you are sick with this *syə'wən*, the help you can get, it can stand you right up and make you walk again. This *syə'wən* it does work, it does save lives where the doctors and hospitals have given up . . . you come into *syə'wən* and your life is saved! (Senior ritualist at initiation ceremony)

The initiator here is a healer by the power of *syə'wən*—just as in Christian tradition the physician is a healer only by the power of God. The traditional Christian theory of the physican's healing power has found a classical expression in the words of the great Paracelsus (1537:172): "on got wird nichts . . . darumb so muss der arzt seine principia im selben auch nemen und on ist er nichts als ein pseudomedicus und ein errant eins fliegenden geists" (Nothing will be achieved without God . . . therefore the physician must take the essential elements of his art from God, and without Him he is nothing but a fake doctor and the errant of a flighty mind). As such an instrument of *syə'wən* the initiating ritualist is empowered to "club to death" the initiate's faulty and diseased old self, to let him awaken with a new potential for total change, and to guide him on the path of Indian tradition through the teachings of his elders. The "new born" initiate is not only called "baby" and "helpless", he is also treated as such: bathed, later fed and dressed, constantly attended and guarded by "babysitters". Regression to a state of complete infantile dependency is at first imposed on the initiate who in the quasi-uterine shelter of the dark longhouse cubicle, hatches his power, prepared to grow with it into a more rewarding and healthier existence. Henceforth, he will count his spiritual age from the day his initiation started. The general belief in death and rebirth through *syə'wən* is reinforced by comments like these:

> I'll tell you what happened to one of my daughters. We clubbed her last winter, she for a fact died, there was no movement in her body, not even a breath, she was stiff as a board. When the spirit came in, it had to change her body, her life, everything changed . . . some people were calling for a doctor from the town, just lack of knowledge of taking care of one that finally travels to the land of *syə'wən* . . . she came back, when she opened up she sang her song. (E.S.)

> They [initiators] kill you as an evil person, they revive you to a new human being, that's why when they club you, you just go and pass out, but you come back . . . there is not to be evil thinking after they're through with you, all you think is I'm starting life all over again. (L.T.)

> It does change your life, just like a rebirth, you feel completely changed, your mind changes, your ways change . . . I was only one month old just now. (Initiate, "grabbed" one month previously.)

> You call a new dancer a baby because he is starting out his life again, they also call him a baby because he is helpless. As a rule we bath the baby . . . You have a funny feeling (as initiate), that's the way they treated you like a newborn. The way they explain this is that you die and wake up to a new life. (L.O.)

> Our young brother stood up to spread his feathers, when he came into *syə'wən* he received a new life, these are our young brother's first steps in his new life. (Ritualist at initiation ceremonial)

Personality Depatterning and Reorientation

The techniques employed today in Spirit dance initiations in the Upper Stalo region are patterned after traditional models pro-

66

vided by the littoral Salish tribes whose ritualists were instrumental in reviving Spirit dancing in the region. In the whole process of initiation, three major therapeutic approaches can be discerned: 1) depatterning through alternating sensory overload and deprivation; followed by 2) physical training with 3) indoctrination.

The candidate is kept in the longhouse, secluded in a dark cubicle or "smokehouse tent" for a period of usually ten days, which in a few privileged cases may be reduced to four days but which may also be prolonged for several weeks, or even for the whole season. The length of this seclusion, which after four days of passive endurance is interrupted by frequent strenuous exercises, varies with candidates and ritualists. It seems to depend mainly on the novice's motivation and his—unconscious or conscious—cooperation in "finding his song and dance" which is the professed purpose of the initiation process. The principal therapeutic functions of this process—personality depatterning and reorientation—are not unknown to the ritualists. In the words of a senior participant:

> It is an Indian treatment, it is a kind of *brainwashing*, four to ten days of torture. Through this torture they soften up, their brain gets soft. During that time you're the weakest and your *brain is back to nil*[2], anything you're taught during those ten days is going to stick with you, you'll never forget it. There is always someone with you during that time, always telling you to change your life. This is when you're taught all rules of your culture . . . the harder the torture the stronger you get. (Y.I.)

Personality depatterning starts with an initial shock treatment known as the "clubbing", "grabbing" or "doctoring up" of the candidate, aiming at rapid induction of an altered state of consciousness, often *via* temporary loss of consciousness. In the cases we witnessed this was the result of a repeated and prolonged treatment which included (a) sudden bodily seizure of the allegedly unexpecting candidate; (b) immobilization of his limbs by physical restraint; (c) blindfolding; (d) hitting, biting and tickling of exposed body parts (abdomen, sides, foot soles) while the candidate was at the same time subjected to (e) kinetic stimulation—uplifted and lowered, hurriedly carried around the longhouse; whirled about and swayed—and to (f) intensive acoustic stimulation—loud drumming and rattling in rapid rhythms, singing and howling close to his ears. This treatment is administered by two teams of eight "workers" taking turns "working" on the candidate under the supervision of the senior ritualist who signals orders by shaking his ceremonial staff. This "grabbing" procedure is repeated at least four times, each time the workers complete four circles around the longhouse hall with their candidate, whose moaning cries become progessively weaker until he appears lifeless, pale and rigid when finally bedded in the cubicle.

When the black-painted ceremonial workers seize him, the candidate is touched or "marked" (E.S.) with a wooden hammer or a ceremonial staff wielded by the ritualist or his assistant. Although this is not more than a gesture, merely imitating the "clubbing to death" of a victim, some candidates react as if they had actually been killed; they immediately fall into motionless rigidity and are lifted up stiff as a board. They usually sing and dance as soon as they wake up from "death". It appears that these candidates had previously shown signs of very severe spirit illness, and that they derive a certain prestige from their instant initiation.

Ritualists and novices comment on these procedures in the following terms:

> You'd put a person down and as soon as you touch him little bit he'd start quivering and die, for hours sometimes; and not only that, he'll start singing right away, that thing was just laying there, ready to come out . . . (E.S.)

> I listen to a person's lungs, I can pick up his song from his body; others [i.e., other ritualists] have to pick it up from his mouth. Then I hum it to the drummers so they can beat the rhythm, and if that's the song, he starts to follow it. The drummers try again, hit the drums harder. If the person is breathing deeply and moving his chest, it's the right song. Later, if the song is repeated, he gets into trance and that's the proof that his song was found. We practice for three nights before we stand him up for dancing. (C.L.)

> You lift him up and hold him up and you blow all over on him the power, it's in your breath. They lose consciousness,

sometimes they are only mumbling the moment they come to. Sometimes you get a person that got a strong will, doesn't give up like, you bath him in hot water, then pour cold water over him. The power part is always there but there are different ways of doing it. On Kuper Island, they spill cold water on you and you pass out. You do it to surprise him, he becomes stiff as a board. (L.O.)

I did not have to be forced to become a dancer, they did not have to chew my sides or to lift me up, he [i.e., the senior ritualist] just touched me with the deerhoof staff and I fell unconscious for about 20 minutes, they say. When I woke up I sang and danced right away. (E.M.)

I did not know that I was going to be a dancer . . . My mother had asked me to go down to the hall and watch, I thought they'd get somebody else . . . Then they came after me, it was such a shock to me. Before they grabbed me I fainted, I just got so scared that I fainted, when I came to I was blindfolded and they had me up in the air. (R.L.)

They (R.L. and N.A.) were clubbed by my cousin, the bear dancer. No trouble clubbing R.L., but lots of trouble with N.A., he fought, they dragged him right from his house to the hall. While they worked on N.A. in the tent, they grabbed R.L., then she hollered once and she passed right out, stiffened right up. They worked on N.A., four times they had to go round the hall with him before he was out. (D.O.)

During his seclusion in the longhouse, the initiate is subjected to physical and psychological treatments for which the terms "torture" and "brainwashing", used by some participants, appear to be quite appropriate, as long as we keep in mind that the purpose is a therapeutic one:

It's a sort of a torture, in order to remember things. I guess it's a life all at once, that is: the tough part of life. We all get our aches and pains through life, so the new dancers get it all on one heap here. (L.T.)

Through the four days of the depatterning phase, the initiate is

69

blindfolded, he has to lie still, is forbidden to talk or to move even in sleep or when sweating under his heavy covers on the fringes of which sit the "babysitters" or "watchmen". He is starved and his fluid intake is restricted; at the same time he is "teased" and "tested" with tasty salmon bits held close to his mouth. Every day he is again exposed to the initial shock of the "grabbing" procedure; he is lifted up and moved around in a chase, he is "tortured"—bitten, hit, tickled and pinched—in order to make him "die" again. The novice's re-entry into the desired altered state of consciousness is facilitated by the ceremonial workers' frequent "singing and drumming to him", not only during the repeated "grabbing" ordeal, but also in front of the immobilized initiate's cubicle, so that the singing might "hit" him. These manoeuvres aim at bringing forth the novice's *song*. They are supplemented by more subtle methods such as placing two eager candidates together with one recalcitrant fellow or by instilling anxiety and guilt feelings:[3]

> When they had me down they could not get me started. Then one old uncle of mine, he came into my tent and started calling me names, trying to make me feel real bad; he said I looked like a rotten log lying there . . . What got me was my granny, I could hear them talking how she gave a shawl and some money for me [for the initiation]. As soon as I heard that I felt like crying, the old lady, about 112 years, thinking of me like that. Things like that they work on a person, will make you feel sad and the song will come. (L.O.)

While lying in his "tent", the initiate perceives his song, dance movements and face-painting in an oneroid state between sleep-dream and wakefulness.[4] It is of utmost importance that both the new dancer and the "workers" know his song and dance correctly, for faulty singing and drumming will be fraught with dangers for the novice. Incorrect face-painting, too, will estrange the guardian spirits:

> My son got the Wolf Song when he was initiated this season. He heard the wolves howling all night when he was initiated, all the others (in the longhouse) heard them, too.

Then he dreamt that his face painting was not right, so he changed it to the right way, and the wolves stopped howling. (Y.I.)

The strict regime of "sacrifices" and "torture" is continued until the initiate "gets his song straight"—usually within four days—to be duly invested then with the traditional "uniform, hat and stick" in sign of his "rebirth in *syə'wən*". The guardian spirit itself—today referred to by the young dancers as the *Indian* or the *Power-Animal*—appears in a "dream" to the novice in the smokehouse cubicle, or in a visionary experience under conditions of physical exertion sometimes in the context of the training which follows the initiate's investiture.

The phase of physical training is associated with intense indoctrination, and is supposed to "make the newborn baby strong". It lasts at least for one week and consists of (a) daily "runs" around the smokehouse hall or outside; often barefoot in snow "to cope with the cold like the oldtimers did"; (b) daily swimming; the new dancers have to jump into the ice-cold waters of Soowahlie Creek, Chilliwack River, Chehalis River, or Cultus Lake, and then to rub their bodies with cedar boughs; (c) frequent rounds of dancing in the smokehouse, to the fast rhythms of many drums which drive the novice to exhaustion.

The following account by an elder presents a genuine picture of the initiation procedures practiced in the Upper Stalo region around 1920:

More than fifty years ago I was just standing there in the smokehouse, did not know what was going to happen. They grab you so fast, so much noise, you can't think much. Twelve husky men come, some grab you and the rest surround you, and they holler with all their might and they rattle them hooves, the drummers they drum, you don't know what happens to you. They strip you down to the waist and they blow on you. I became so frightened that I lost control of myself. Whether I hollered, I don't know. It gets so that you are out of breath, you kind of get unconscious. I could hear them, but I could not see them; they blindfold you so you can't see what's going on. There is so many singers there and different guys drumming; it kind of

71

carries your mind away, it comes to your head and this causes the change in you. You hear the song, it's in your ears, and finally you come out with it . . . After I became a dancer I could hear singing from all directions. I could hear the trees sing, the movements of the trees rubbing together, I could hear the birds sing; anywhere I looked in the forest it became a song. They used to tell us, when you go out to the bush don't take a song, wait until it comes to you, you hear it long ways. I just had to go to the forest and I got a song. But now I've been a dancer for over fifty years. I don't hear the singing in the forest anymore . . . (C.L.)

The immediate subjective experience of a contemporary initiate is conveyed in this report by an Indian girl:

They use the old dancers to work on you because they've got the power, and they bite on your side to put their power inside you. You feel a lot of pain when they work on you; when they bite you, you have to scream and holler, and pretty soon your song comes. I felt the pain in my stomach where they bit me, they tighten it and then they pull on it, and then your song comes out stronger. Then they slap you really hard on the stomach . . . I passed out about three times while they worked on me, they kept doing that to me every morning and every night for four days, on the fourth day they just lifted me up and blew on me all over. It's just after they work on you the song comes to you, you hear it and you sing it, it was the second day that I heard mine, and it came on the third night. It was the third day that I saw how my face was to be painted, it was in my sleep, in a dream, I saw the way I was supposed to dance; I saw myself and I heard my song. Then they put the hat and uniform on you and then take your stick, when you start to sing the stick just moves to the beat of your song and that's how they get to drum for you. You have to sing your song because it comes to you, you can hear it and you voice it, but it's something else, not you, that makes you voice it. For four days they don't feed you nothing, we were in our tents, you can hear them eating outside, it bothers you. After the fourth day they give you the salmon and you

72

have to just spit it back out; even if you wanted to, you couldn't eat it, it would make you sick. I felt like throwing up, only I did not have anything in my stomach. You have to go swimming every morning, usually go up Chilliwack Lake. The first couple of times it's real cold but you've your power and you get strong, the water doesn't bother you, your power protects you. Sometimes after we came from swimming they run us in the hall, or we went for a run or go for a long walk, and sometimes you see something there. Your babysitter, that one that watches you all the time, don't see anything, just yourself. We call it your Indian, everybody's is different, it's your Power-Animal, but you could see anything, like one's got the Lizard, partly animal, partly human; another's got the Ocean Animal, a black fish. (R.L.)

Released from their incubation, the initiates feel their newly acquired power when the song bursts forth from them and the leaping steps of their first dance carry them through the long-house, spurred on by the rhythms of deerhide drums and the chanting and clapping of the crowd. One new dancer likened this blissful experience to that of a chemically induced altered state of consciousness:

I was jumping three feet high and I had such a thrill, a terrific feeling as if you were floating, as if you were in the air, you feel really high. I've only had such a feeling once before in my life when I was on heroin mainlining, but then I went through hell afterwards, it was terrible—but with syə'wən you get this feeling without the terrible aftermath. (E.M.)

Perhaps the most pertinent description of the altered state of consciousness experienced by spirit dancers was given by an Indian elder who has gone through what he himself calls a "trance" many times while dancing:

It seems to me this power is like electricity; that's why I would not let anybody dance behind me, not even my son. It's a force that makes you dance, something like a shock;

when you are sitting there you feel a real jolt that makes you jump up and dance. They used to tell us—the baby-sitters as they are now called—when you are about to get into a trance, breath hard, real hard, don't hold it back; if you do you're liable to faint. Breath hard from down here, from your stomach, all out. So you breathe deep; your whole body, chest and stomach is moving.[5] You get into trance before you jump up and dance. If you are in a real trance, your muscles get really strong and your body gets hard as a board. Just as soon as you come into trance, even if you are not blindfolded, there is a shield coming down over your eyes so that you don't see anything. When you are in a trance you just hear your song and the drums, you don't see anything. If you're really in trance you wouldn't run into the fire or fall down, your spirit guide will not let you do this. But we don't take any chances with the babies, that's why we have the fire watchers . . . The first time I went around the smokehouse hall I didn't know where I was going, but I could sense the people. You always turn to the left, never to the right; so in turning to the left you go right around the hall, and when you come to the finish it seems you're kind of slackening off. First thing you glance at is the seat where you were, that's why you never miss the seat, 'cause you have already sensed the people. . . Some of the guys that have been drinking say you feel like this when you were high on booze and you come out of it, they say it's just like if you sober up. Well, I don't know because I don't drink. It just seems to me I wake up, suddenly you are back to reality. (C.L.)

In view of Neher's (1960) findings on the neurophysio-logical effects of rhythmic drumming (*vide supra*, 19-20), this type of sensory stimulation, so very prominent in Salish spirit dancing, has to be considered as a major factor operating in the induction of altered states of consciousness during spirit dance initiation. Physical analysis of records of drumming[6] during local ceremonies in the 1970-71 season, reveals that rhythmic drum-ming encompasses a frequency range from 0.8 to 5.0 cps, with a mean frequency of 2.95 cps. One-third of the recorded frequen-cies are above 3.0 cps, i.e. within, or close to the frequency of the theta waves of the human electroencephalogram. Frequencies in this range are entirely predominant in drumming during initiation procedures. As the reader may recall, Neher (1960) demonstrated *auditory driving* in the EEG of all subjects exposed to one percussion instrument of a type very similar to the Salish deer skin drum. He also elicited various subjective responses, some of them corresponding to those reported in altered states of consciousness. As a stimulus frequency in the theta range of the EEG (four to seven cycles per second) is expected to be most effective in the production of trance states, Neher assumed drumming rhythms close to such frequencies to be preponderant in ceremonies associated with trance behaviour. It need not be emphasized that rhythmic acoustic stimulation in this ceremonial is far more intensive than in Neher's experiments: not one, but many drums are employed. Indeed, the effects of rhythmic drumming may contribute to the "contagiousness" of a spirit power which often seizes uninitiated persons present at ceremonials.

Let us now turn to the didactic aspects of spirit dance initiation. Modern spirit dancers refer to the initiation as a salutary learning experience: "It teaches you physical, emotional, and mental well-being." (L.S.) While much of this learning is effected through non-verbal conditioning processes, theoretical indoctrination also plays an important role. It includes (a) the direct teaching of the rules and sanctions of *syə'wən*, and (b) the indirect reinforcement of collective suggestion by recounting of *syə'wən*— lore, presenting examples of the works of spirit, or "spiritual", power. Furthermore, it also includes (c) what may be called culture propaganda; we shall deal with this interesting aspect of *syə'wən* teaching later. Theoretical indoctrination takes place in the smokehouse cubicle as a personally focused persuasion, and *coram populo* when ceremonial speakers publicly address the new dancers assembled in the longhouse. The main agents of formal indoctrination are the ritualists. In our experience, the senior ritualists display considerable skill in suggestive psychotherapy and in overcoming the client's resistance. It was no exaggeration when one of these therapists asserted:

> Being with people I can size them up and tell 'em words
> that's needed . . . If there's going to be the slightest doubt
> it's no use working [on candidates], so you got to make

them aware of what will or should take place, because it's
bad enough to work on a sick person, let alone the doubt—
in other words, you got to have one mind in anything you
do in order to succeed. By this teaching, we'd fix a person
to sing; club him, pack him around, sit him down and he'll
sing; we'll take care of him step by step, so people will look
up to it and they'll think well, there must be something in
the Indian.

When teaching the new dancers, the ritualists speak with ancestral
spiritual authority, they "have to reflect the word of our old
people." (E.S.) Among the *syə'wən* rules taught are traditional
prescriptions and proscriptions regarding avoidance of menstruating women; ways of talking, eating and drinking, which are
today subject to various rationalizations (for example, avoid the
intake of hot or ice-cold liquids in order to protect your teeth;
avoid looking at the sun in order to protect your eyes). More
relevant to behavioural reorientation is the instilling in the initiate
of a sense of personal responsibility towards his elders and his
people:

We tell the young people the other tribes will look at us,
they'll say those people don't know how to bring up their
new dancers. We don't want the other tribes talking about
us and that's why the rules are strict ... they are supposed
to be binding for one year anyway. (L.O.)

Resting on the shoulders of this man [initiate] is the reputation of all you people, all the tribe of Chilliwack, all the
people that went before him. This is why you are instructed
to take care of this in *syə'wən*. Once you open your mouth
to *syə'wən* you are not to have a mean bone in your body,
you are not to use these hands to hurt any of your people,
you are not to use this voice to hurt any other dancer's
feelings! (Senior ritualist addressing new dancer)

As a dancer, you feel responsible to all the people, you
feel guilty if you don't keep the rules; you harm the whole
group that you belong to. (Y.I.)

The new dancer is, above all, obliged to "respect *syə'wən*" by not

76

revealing anything about it to outsiders; he has to do honour to his elders by behaving "decently", and to faithfully observe the ceremonial by attending as many dances as he can. Of utmost therapeutic importance is the prohibition of alcohol intake (and also of smoking and illicit drugs). The alcohol taboo is supposed to be valid for all active dancers during syə'wən season; but is strictly enforced only for the initiates while they are in uniform, i.e. throughout the season of their initiation, although they are expected to stay away from liquor at least for one year. It appears noteworthy that prohibition of alcohol did not originate from considerations of health and welfare, but from the need to outlaw disruptive behaviour:

> It was a rule in them days that you are not supposed to make a fool of yourself or make fun of anybody ... We did not allow any drunken people, so they made it a rule that when you are drunk you are not supposed to come in. You got so used to it, so you never drink anyway. (Traditional dancer)

Whereas abuse of alcohol by all participants during syə'wən season is strongly discouraged and frowned upon, off-season abstention is not emphasized. Nevertheless, the achievement even of seasonal abstention through spirit dancing would be of considerable public health significance for the Indian population of British Columbia.[7]

Besides these general syə'wən rules there are individual rules of conduct for each new dancer, taking into account the particular problems by which his initiation was motivated. The theme of total personality change, intrinsic to the therapeutic myth of death and rebirth, is repeated in the ritualists' public admonitions of individual novices.

Observance of general and individual syə'wən rules is enforced by (a) social and (b) supernatural sanctions. During the initiation period, the "babysitters" or "watchmen" have to supervise the novice's behaviour, but also to protect him:

> The watchman has to watch him all the time, wherever he goes, see that he don't smoke or drink or break the rules.

Not only that, the new dancer might get frightened and get startled and he'll run ... that's why the watchman is there. (L.O.)

Equally, or probably more effective in keeping the new dancer in line, is the group pressure exerted on him. A novice who reneges by leaving the ceremonial and breaking the *syə'wən* rules is not only inviting supernatural retaliation and all kinds of social troubles—into which he invariably gets as expected—but also rejection by his group:

That girl ran away after she was initiated, so now she's gone from bad to worse, she got into all kinds of trouble recently, she has three charges and now she got into a car accident. She becomes almost the black sheep in the family, the other dancers shun her if she don't stick to the rules ... but still if she does return it's their rule that they've got to accept her again and try to help her. (Y.I.)

A highly efficient group sanction is a shaming procedure, the threat of which usually suffices to ensure better compliance with rules. If a young dancer continues to misbehave, his sponsors warn him they are going to invite people to a *potlatch*, where prominent leaders will elaborate on his wrongdoings and "preach" to him, which is felt to be a public shame.

To violate the rules means to insult *syə'wən*, and this brings all kinds of harm upon the culprit, and also upon those close to him. Ritualists and old dancers testify to *syə'wən's* retaliatory power by reporting stories of its vengeance. *Syə'wən* may "go away" from deviant dancers and "leave people like that the biggest tramps there is". *Syə'wən* is said to have punished defectors by causing their children to die; to have inflicted illness or other bodily harm on those who infringed upon its rules; or to have prevented songs to issue from the guilty ones while at the same time giving them a painful urge to sing. At ceremonial occasions, the new dancers are admonished to be genuine and sincere in their belief in, and practice of, *syə'wən*, and to fear its revenge:

I know what *syə'wən* means to me. I must live the life my

78

ancestors want me to, I don't make a show out of *syə'wən*. That's the way my grandfather taught me before he went, he told me 'Son, I don't want you to make mockery out of *syə'wən*, don't you ever make fun out of *syə'wən* because it can cut off your life right now, it can get along without you just as well as it can get along with you'. So therefore that's what I hope, that you believe in the things you will tell to your grandchildren. (Indian Doctor's address, Tzeachten)

The initiation process ends with the disrobing ceremony. The new dancer is supposed to stay in his initiation garb until the end of the season during which he was "grabbed". However, exceptions are made today for vocational reasons, not without the ritualist's public announcement of the initiate's pledge to observe the rules of *syə'wən* and to "keep on singing until the season is over". At the disrobing ceremony, witnesses are called up to "help this young man here to strip his uniform, take off his belt and his pole"; for their symbolic assistance witnesses receive kerchiefs as "souvenirs". The ritualist and workers who gave the "newborn baby" his first bath, take the bathing utensils as their share. The ceremony is concluded with speeches by ritualists and witnesses who address the initiate by his Indian name.

The therapeutic implication of this ceremony is that it documents the candidate's successful cure from spirit illness through a duly performed intiation treatment. Together with his uniform, the initiate sheds the last vestiges of his old personality as the snake sloughs off its old skin. The new dancer is presented to the public as yet another testifier to the healing and regenerating power of *syə'wən*. In the words of the ritualists:

T. [Indian name of initiate] is the one standing here, as you know he was a very sick man, he was unable to move, and now you see the difference; the change that has taken him into his *syə'wən* life has made a new man out of him. T. wants to thank each and everyone for coming together at his party to take off his uniform, that's the reason why you are asked to witness what we have done, to witness that he stripped his uniform, so nobody can say anything. Next year you'll hear of T. again!

79

If you did not complete this season and take off this uniform, you'd feel dizzy like you're going to fall. There is some that I know that did not finish like this; they have this sickness and they will carry it for the rest of their lives. Now that you have come this far, when your uniform is taken off everyone of the bad habits you had, if you listened, is going to go. You are going to come out a brand new man! So prove to your people that there is something in *syǝ'wǝn*, because this *syǝ'wǝn* proved it to you now! From now on to the end of your life take care of this gift that was given to you! (Senior ritualists at ceremonial, Wellington Reserve)

It is not before he has duly observed his duties as a new dancer for four years after initiation, that a person becomes fully established in the ceremonial and is considered capable of assuming important assistant roles in initiation procedures. If he is entitled to wear the traditional human hair and feathers headdress, this will be ceremonially bestowed on him in the fourth year of his "life in *syǝ'wǝn*" as an outward sign of his maturity.

Indications for Initiation and Selection of Candidates

Senior ritualists working in the region recognize the following types of legitimate candidacy for spirit dance initiation:
1) Volunteering, with or without spirit illness.
2) Spirit illness.
3) Behaviour harmful to self and/or others.
   Various forms of psycho- and socio-pathology are considered in this latter category:

It's when you don't regard your life. You mistreat yourself and those around you, and probably you're going to be a candidate for suicide. People will see this and will say it would be safer if you come in *syǝ'wǝn* and change your life. (E.S.)

When questioned for examples of candidates belonging in this category, informants referred to cases of (a) manifest and chronic

80

depressive symptomatology; (b) antisocial acting-out behaviour with alcohol and drug abuse; (c) adjustment problems of adolescence; (d) maltreatment of spouse—in that order of decreasing frequency.

(4) Mockery of the ceremonial or provocation of participants. There are numerous instances of unconscious self-selection by quasi-defiant persons who engage in the very acts they know will make them liable to social and supernatural punishment by imposed initiation. These candidates are mostly young men displaying aggressive attitudes. With all their bragging of alleged immunity to *syə'wən* power, their ambivalently expressed motivation is, of course, apparent to the ritualists: "That's one way of saying 'I want to become a dancer, too' "; "the more you fight it, the better dancer you'll be". Indeed, cases of this description which we observed (one fellow dared the ritualists to "grab" him; another mocked the ritual and announced he would defend himself with a hatchet, yet another threatened to shoot whoever would try to discipline him through initiation) turned out to become most active participants in the ceremonial and ardent believers in *syə'wən* power. Besides assuming a strong unconscious motivation in these cases we have to take into account that their defiant posturing exposes them to an especially severe initiation treatment. One of the most recalcitrant candidates, now quite vocal in praising the merits of spirit dancing, had to be "dragged" to the longhouse and was subjected to more intensified high frequency drumming than the other initiates.

Young women sometimes reveal their ambivalent motivation by demonstrative curiosity about *syə'wən* while they profess their disinclination to become dancers. This also is generally interpreted as camouflaged volunteering:

> They more or less would like to see how it works, they are very interested in it and yet say they don't want it. Once the Indian Doctor realizes that, he says well she wants it and we might just as well give it to her. (L.T.)

(5) Being the spouse or the prospective spouse of a dancer or initiate. This is looked upon as a valid reason for initiation in order to bolster marital harmony, especially if other indications are also present. In the case of young couples or fiancés,

joint induction may be deemed advisable from a realistic point of view:

> It is usually best to take young people together that are starting to invite; we figure if we take him we'll take her, too, so there wouldn't be any hard feelings between him and her. If we didn't take her she might start running around because [during initiation] he is not allowed to go anywhere. (Senior ritualist)

Whatever the reasons for someone to be considered a candidate for spirit dancing, unless he is sponsored his initiation is unlikely to ever take place. In the Upper Stalo region today, a candidate is supposed to have individual and personal sponsor(s). Anonymous sponsoring through collections ("putting down the drum in the smokehouse") is apparently permissible in special cases, but not practiced here. Senior ritualists feel that "somebody has to stand behind a person as an anchor"; and "even if you volunteer you have to have somebody there to take care of you". When exploring the grounds on which some volunteers are rejected, the basic objection in these cases turns out to be that there was no "good solid sponsor" behind them. The sponsor, usually a parent, senior relative or close friend of the family, assumes paedagogic as well as financial responsibilities: he must be capable and willing to back up the initiators, encouraging or, if necessary, enforcing the candidate's cooperation in the treatment procedures of initiation. The outcome of the initiation process depends to a considerable degree on the sponsor's attitude; his lack of firmness may encourage the candidate to "drop out", as in the case of two girls during the 1971-72 season. The sponsor may, therefore, be looked upon as the guarantor of therapeutic success, and the importance attributed to him by the ritualists bespeaks their realistic judgement.

The following summary of pre-initiation behaviour and symptom formation is based on twenty-four "modern" spirit dancers on whom relevant data could be obtained from reliable sources. This sample encompasses between 50% and 80% of those initiated since the revival of spirit dancing in the Upper Stalo region from 1967 to 1972. No reliable data indicating the presence of psychic or behavioural pre-initiation problems could be obtained on further ten of the thirty-four identified "modern"

82

dancers (total number of active spirit dancers in the Upper Stalo region in 1972 is estimated at between 40 to 50).

Predominant symptom formation before spirit dance initiation:

In 11 candiates:	In 13 candidates:
Depression, anxiety, psychogenic somatization often associated with alcohol and/or drug abuse.	Behaviour problems with aggressive or antisocial tendencies, usually associated with alcohol and/or drug abuse.

Costs and Risks

In many cultures, including those of the Western world, treatment expenses are of considerable therapeutic relevance especially in disorders of psychogenic nature. Frequently, the investment in a patient's cure can be said to be directly related to its success, if the investment is the patient's own or that of persons meaningful to him. A consideration of the costs of *syə'wən* is therefore also part of an exploration of its therapeutic aspects.

The total expenditure for the initiation of one candidate is said to be between $1,000 and $2,000 for the whole season, or about $20 for each gathering. This sum includes expenses for feeding many guests many times; gifts and payments to "workers" and "babysitters", "souvenirs" for the "witnesses", etc.

Traditionally, this was paid in kind and by giving away woven goods or Hudson's Bay Company blankets. Handicrafts of the donor's own make are still highly appreciated as gifts or souvenirs but have become rare. In the Upper Stalo region, obligations towards those who assisted in the initiation ceremonials are expected to be met until the end of the next winter season. Compensation for the—actual or symbolic—services rendered to the initiates of the previous season is part of the annual winter dance ceremonial, an elaborate ritual of public display and giving-away of stacks of blankets and other items. This part of the winter ceremonial, the so-called "work", is more than just reminiscent of the traditional Northwest Coast *potlatch*, it is also often referred to as such by the participants.

For many Indian families in the Valley these expenses mean considerable financial hardships, and may, therefore, discourage some from "giving away" their sons and daughters. Quite a few, however, would argue, "Do you think our religion and our higher

83

power isn't worth $2,000? It's worth more than that." (L.T.)
For those initiates who hold jobs throughout the year, the material sacrifice is substantial. However, they are a small minority because the predominantly seasonal type of employment in the area puts the greater part of Indian manpower out of work in winter time, an economic factor which certainly facilitated the revival of spirit dancing in the Upper Stalo region. Non-financial risks are also associated with spirit dance initiations. In the case of young mothers, the children's welfare has to be considered, and ritualists will be reluctant to accept such candidates unless adequate provision for child care has been made.

In spite of the very stressful procedures the novices are subjected to, no serious accident occurred during initiation procedures in the Upper Stalo region in the period of observation 1967-72. Four new dancers had to be admitted to medical-surgical wards of Chilliwack General Hospital in the course of their initiation, for the following reasons:

January 1971; woman age 18; on admission acute abdominal pain; diagnosis—cholecystitis.

December 1971; woman age 19; on admission chilly, shivery, coughing, abdominal tenderness; diagnosis—bronchitis; exposure and psychological stress reaction.

December 1971; woman age 19; on admission cold, tired, hungry, sore knee, scratchmarks on abdomen; diagnosis—soft tissue injury of right knee joint; skin lesions, possible human bites; exhaustion.

February 1972; man age 20; on admission pain, sweating, edematous swelling and numbness of both feet and ankles; diagnosis—frostbite.

None of the above patients dropped out of the initiation program. A *skwəni'ləc* healing ceremony was performed for the girl who had to have cholecystectomy, the patient's "uniform" taking her place in this ritual while she was in hospital. The participants were convinced that this would help and the patient herself told us she felt great relief. At any rate, her recovery was speedy. In parenthesis it may be mentioned that one male initiate died in circulatory collapse at LaConner, Washington, during the ceremonial season 1970-71; he is reported to have suffered from a chronic cardiac condition unbeknownst to the ritualists.

84

Footnotes

1. The term *ritualist* as used in this book refers to persons holding prestige among the Coast Salish people, as elders and leading functionaries officiating at the spirit dance ceremonial. The usage of the term is not identical with that by Barnett (1955:129) who makes a clear distinction between *shaman-doctor* and *priest-ritualist*. However, such definitive distinctions do not appear to obtain today in Coast Salish society.

2. This very idea was expressed by John Locke (1632-1714) in his *tabula rasa* concept: at birth the mind is a blank slate upon which impressions are recorded by experience. Locke would presumably have postulated the mind to become a *tabula rasa* again in any genuine rebirth. Compare also Sargant's (1959) observations on religious and ideological conversion techniques *(vide supra)*, he reports that an Evangelist sect in the U.S.A. refers to their type of brainwashing as "wiping the slate clean for God".

3. Cf. Sargant (1959:130); "Brain-washers use a technique of conversion which does not depend only on the heightening of group suggestibility, but also on the fomenting in an individual of anxiety, of a sense of real or imaginary guilt . . . strong and prolonged enough to bring about the desired collapse."

4. Reminiscent of the therapeutic dream-revelations to patients during incubation in the Aesculapian Temples of Healing of ancient Greece.

5. Note the use of hyperventilation (forced rapid and deep breathing), a universally known and time-honoured method of inducing altered states of consciousness.

6. For this physical analysis we are indebted to Dr. Helmut Ormestad of the Fysisk Institutt Blindern of the University of Oslo, Norway.

7. For the contributing role of alcohol in the alarmingly high accidental death rates among British Columbia Indians see Schmitt et al. (1966), and the report on mortality statistics by the Federal Health Service, for the year 1972. (The Indian Voice, February 1974:1,12)

Chapter Six

Annual Winter Therapy

Although the number of active spirit dancers is still relatively small in the Upper Stalo region, the winter ceremonials already now involve the majority of the native population in some way or other: the relatives or friends of dancers, or other invited guests. Not only for those who have become active dancers through initiation and continue to dance at the gatherings of each subsequent season, but also for their relatives and for many other Indian families, the winter time now brings every year an immersion in group activities, which in scope and duration is unparalleled in non-Indian society. As some participation is expected from the audience, too, the ceremonial holds more than entertainment value even for the casual spectator.

In the Upper Fraser Valley, winter unemployment is prevalent not only among the Indian population. The association of such imposed idleness with marital and intrafamily conflicts, alcohol, narcotic and psychedelic drug abuse, increasing demands for medical attention and hospitalization due to psychogenic symptom formation, is obvious to all social agencies and health professionals in the area. In this situation, the holding of spirit dances throughout the winter season represents a most valuable annual therapeutic enterprise for the benefit of the local Indian population. This enterprise integrates the following therapeutic techniques:

Occupational and activity therapy;
Group psychotherapy;
Cathartic abreaction;
Psychodrama;
Direct ego-support;
Physical exercise.

Before discussing our own observations on these techniques in Upper Stalo spirit dancing, let us again refer to pertinent ethnographic reports.

There are many references in the ethnographic literature which unmistakably report native views of spirit dancing as a means of annual restoration or preservation of physical and emotional wellbeing. It is certainly significant that the Salish winter spirit ceremonials are often associated with specific shamanistic curing performances such as the *sbEtEtda'q* of the Puget Sound tribes (Haeberlin 1918); the *skʷəni'ləč* procedures we have seen in local dances (*vide infra*) and which were previously observed at Musqueam by Kew (1970); or the healing rite recorded by Lerman (1954) in the Okanagan. More generally, however, it is part of Salish ideology that spirit dancing and singing in itself have curative and prophylactic effects on the participants. The Flathead Indians viewed their winter medicine dance as preventing sickness and destroying "bad medicine" (Teit 1930); Shuswap mystery singing was done to discover illness, bewitchment and evil, and to boost the self-confidence of the young. (Teit 1905) Musqueam dancers gather in sympathy for sorrowing or bereaved persons to "help them sing"; spirit dance initiation is felt to be beneficial to health. (Kew 1970) Spirit songs may come unsought to Lummi Indians in grief, and spirit singing after a tragedy is known to give a feeling of well-being. (Suttles 1954)

Several observers have underlined the psychotherapeutic role of spirit dancing. Thus, Kew (1970) notes the unanimous group support for the participant who often manifests a violent expression of anguish and despair; Stern (1934) remarks on the women dancers' display of, and thereby relief from, marital distress; Wike (1941) relates how gestures of activities characteristic of physical well-being, associated with particular spirits, are utilized in the dances of the Swinomish. It is foremost the emotionally and materially deprived who become singers among the Swinomish: "You use that song to straighten the mind like a prayer to live, like doctoring your mind." (Wike 1941:41) There can indeed be no doubt about the psychotherapeutic value of the Warrior Dance if enacted by a discouraged and depressed young girl, nor about the ego-strengthening effect of the proud Warrior Song:

I am great
I am great
It's true that I am great." (Wike, 1941:78)

The induction of alcoholics into the winter dance ceremonial is understood in terms of cure rather than punishment by the

Cowichan. (Lane 1953) The Puyallup-Nisqually feel the spirit power's satisfaction through dance ceremonies is necessary for individual and collective well-being. (Smith 1940) We realize, therefore, why Suttles (1963:519) views spirit dancing as "attempts by individuals and kin groups to maintain psychic integrity and social status", and why Robinson (1963:126) sees it as a "kind of therapy devised to prevent as well as cure general malaise or mitigate excessive grief or anxiety."

The *occupational—and activity-therapeutic* function of spirit dancing in the vocational off-season of the Upper Stalo region is evident from what was outlined earlier. Excerpts from a probation officer's case report illustrate the importance of full-time occupation with the ceremonial, in the rehabilitation of young Indian offenders:

> When looking at Subject's schooling and work record, one is left with the impression that subject is lazy and lacking goals or direction . . . Subject has become actively involved in the Indian dancing rituals. This has taken up most of his time since December and he is absent from home for most of the weekends.

One year later:

> Subject's behaviour considerably improved, no further offences, no evidence of alcohol or drug use.

The principles of *group therapy* (Frank and Powdermaker 1959) are operant in the spirit dance ceremonial: it provides the participant with support, protection, acceptance, and stimulation. Perhaps the most relevant group-therapeutic aspect of the winter dance ceremonial is that the participant is turned from egocentric preoccupations to collective concerns and the pursuit of collective goals: "The special relevance of dependency of man on society in this context is to direct man's individual strivings toward partly collective goals." (Aberle 1972)[1] Group solidarity is stressed in speeches held during ceremonial gatherings. Non-dancing participants contribute to the success of the ceremonial as much as the active dancers. Not only are non-dancers involved in organizing the dances and making the uniforms, in longhouse maintenance, tending the fires, and catering the meals, etc., many of them drum and sing for hours, accompanying one dancer after another on his counterclockwise dancing tour around the longhouse hall; others shield the tranced dancers from the fire or help them back to their seats. Those in the audience clap hands or beat sticks in time which the dancer's chant. They all share in the responsibility of satisfying *syə'wən*, lest it might be angered by faulty rhythms or some other irregularity and then bring harm upon the dancer and his people:

> There is a way in which you can mistreat the spirit, and some don't know enough to take care of the spirit, enough for him to stay and really help somebody; not only that, as a help for the whole group, the whole tribe. (Senior ritualist)

In the case of an unforeseen event—such as once when a dancer's ceremonial staff was dropped—the affected person's kin group and friends immediately take action, undoing the occurrence by appropriate ritual action and announcing their obligation for assistance and testimony through the ritualist. Participation in the ceremonial, by dancers and non-dancers alike, is often motivated by the strong group support they experience:

> My sons feel like belonging to a great club now, they have friends everywhere in the Salish area, they all consider themselves brothers and sisters. When they enter a longhouse they know they belong to all these people. That gives them security, a sense of belonging. (Y.I.)

Indeed, there is no loneliness in *syə'wən*; the mutual interest of the participants in each other is renewed every year. As the ritualist assures at the end of the season:

> Remember, next year *syə'wən* will be looking for you, for everyone here someone will be looking for! (Tzeachten, 1971)

The use of a group-psychotherapeutic approach can also be clearly seen in the *skʷənilə̌c* procedure, a shamanistic curing rite which has become part of the annual spirit dance ceremonial in

89

the Upper Stalo region, performed only on special occasions by the same Lummi "Indian Doctor". The audience is called upon by the Indian Doctor to render active assistance through mental concentration on the patient in order to "help him". During the healing manipulations, the patient is surrounded by relatives and friends, who support him affectionately and accompany him home. In the rituals we observed (Rosedale, March 1970 and Tzeachten, January 1971), the violent force of the power-charged paraphernalia[2] was demonstrated to the public before they were used as therapeutic tools: two pairs of husky assistants, each pair holding on to one instrument with all their might, were unable to tame its wildness. As drums beat fast rhythms and women sacrificed food by throwing it into the fire, the two instruments seemed to swiftly drag their bearers through the hall. Pulling together with irresistible magnetic attraction, the powerful tools could only be severed again and handled by the Indian Doctor himself. Soon the instruments moved toward the persons singled out for treatment, gently stroking along the heads and bodies of the clients. At one time, the focus of therapeutic effort was a recalcitrant initiate with serious behaviour problems; on another occasion it was a patient of ours. This latter case deserves special mention, having had the attention of various physicians, and eight hospital admissions from 1967 to 1970 with severe neurotic and psychosomatic symptom formation, including three suicidal attempts in depressive reactions. Shortly after the healing rite, the patient, who had been anorectic and insomnic, stated:

> I don't remember much, it was like a nightmare, I was not really conscious but I felt something like power. I don't know how I came home, fell asleep right away. I woke up in the morning and felt stronger. The first thing was I was hungry. I really felt the power, a great big load taken off my shoulders.

The patient became a regular participant in the winter ceremonials and has been able to function without rehospitalization since 1970, in spite of severe outside stress.

Cathartic abreaction is defined by Bleuler (1960:144) as an affective abreaction "aiming at the liberation from emotional tension by the affectively charged act of remembering and re-living the situation in which the tension was generated". Such an abreaction will be a therapeutic experience for the patient if bystanders show total acceptance and benevolent empathy. This situation obtains at the winter spirit ceremonial: the learning experience of initiation enables the dancer to re-enter an altered state of consciousness without initiatory preparation; and in this state he re-lives the coming of his song which then breaks forth from him in a tremendous affective and motor discharge, in front of an interested and helpful audience. Throughout the ceremonial season, these affective discharges take place at every spirit dance gathering. Hundreds of spectators watch a young mother tremble, sob and moan, then hand her baby to a neighbour and leap up into a wild dance with a final *arc de cercle* before she is carefully guided back to her seat, still sobbing but soon cheerful and reaching for her child; or a stout man, jumping high and light-footed in his dance, blaring out his song open-mouthed and throwing his arms vehemently as if pushing everyone aside. Although *syə'wən* is supposed to make its established round as announced by the ritualist, possessing one dancer after another, the drummers will come to a young dancer's assistance who, as yet unable to control the power, is shaking violently, rattling the deer-hoof staff and blurting out the song; or is howling and writhing on the bench, to be pacified only by an extra-curricular dance out of turn. The tension-releasing effect of "singing out one's song" is akin to that of crying:[3]

> In *syə'wən* you are supposed to cry . . . it helps me, I sing and I cry, and I feel better afterwards." (L.S.)
> "The old-timers used to express their feelings in tunes and movements. All the dancers still do this . . . if you go to a funeral, the old dancers, they cry and it changes to song, same song as in the dances. (L.O.)

By expressing his affects in a recognized and ritualized form to a sympathetic audience, the dancer learns to accept his emotions and at the same time, to control them. A senior ritualist put it this way:

> The spirit is there, the thing is to accept it by voicing it to

somebody; it's going to be well received by the people that's going to hear it, and it's going to be taken care of.

Psychodrama. Dramatic acting-out is a most conspicuous feature of the spirit dancers' performance in the ceremonial. Self-expressive dramatization of affects through the personification of supernatural beings who are culturally at hand for ritual possessions, so to speak, has been utilized for psychotherapeutic purposes in many cultures. As a paradigm of such ceremonial therapy, Haitian *Voodoo* is the favourite subject of ethnopsychiatric investigation.[4] Yap (1960) provides us with a useful formulation of the function of dramatic acting out in the transcultural "possession syndrome", which he studied in the context of Hong King Chinese culture.[5] He notes the powerful psychological effect on the audience of the mythological *dramatis personae* entering the stage of the Chinese popular opera through the so-called "Ghost Door", and relates a tradition of actors being possessed by the spirits they impersonate. At the Salish winter ceremonial, each spirit dancer repeats his first *syə'wən* possession, at every dance he again becomes possessed, i.e. he re-enters a trance-like state in order to feel and display the personal spirit power originally acquired in the altered state of consciousness induced by initiation procedures. Some dancers are experienced virtuosi in achieving such a state; they work themselves up with loud hyperventilation and vehement commotion, to pass into song and dance when dozens of deer-hide drums strike in. The dancer's spirit finds its dramatized expression in dance steps, tempo, movements, miens and gestures: in the sneaking pace, then flying leaps of the ferociously yelling "warrior", or in the swaying trot of the plump, sadly weeping "bear mother"; in the rubber-like reptilian writhing of the "double headed serpent" as well as in the desperate wailing and gesticulation of the "mother seeking her child"; just as in the "lizard" who sheds tears over his devoured offspring or in the mighty "whale" who grabs smaller fish.

The choreographic drama of the spirit dance is *therapeutic psychodrama*, by virtue of its combination with a cathartic abreaction in an appropriate group setting. It is certainly not coincidental that the founder of modern psychodramatic therapy himself drew parallels between shamanistic transactions of North

American Indians and psychodramatic sessions. (Moreno 1959) His definition of psychodramatic action as a therapeutic, controlled acting-out taking place under the guidance of therapists in a safe treatment setting (Moreno 1955) is applicable to the winter spirit ceremonial. We recognize in the spirit dance participants the *dramatis personae* of Moreno's clinical psychodrama: protagonists (the dancers), auxiliary egos (babysitters or assistants), director (ritualist) and group (audience). Mumford's dictum (1951), "psychodrama is the essence of the dream", will remind us of the *syə'wən* teaching that spirit song, face painting, and dance movements are revealed to the novice in a dream. Psychic purification or *catharsis* was first perceived as a function of drama by Aristotle (384-322 B.C.) in his "Poetics", where drama is characterized as the imitation of an action which by arousing sympathy and fear effects a purification, i.e. catharsis, of the spectators' affects.[6] Modern spontaneous psychodrama, on the other hand, intends to achieve cathartic abreaction in the actors:

It [psychodrama] produces a healing effect—not in the spectator . . . but in the producer—actors who produce the drama and, at the same time, liberate themselves from it. (Moreno 1923)

We do not consider it presumptuous to conclude from our observation of Coast Salish spirit dancing that it combines Aristotle's and Moreno's criteria by providing for affective catharsis, both in spectators and actors.

Ego-support accrues out of the group-therapeutic and cathartic-psychodramatic facets of spirit dancing. *Direct ego-support* results from the positive attention the ritualist leaders and the people focus on the active dancers throughout the winter ceremonial:

Many people are going to see your face tonight. You might say the people do not know me, but everybody will know you tonight. We, the Lummi people, the LaConner people, the Musqueam people, the Chilliwack people, will all know you! Before you came into *syə'wən*, you were sitting behind, no one knew who you was. Your people put you out in front, and they stand behind you, all the people now know your names. . . .

We are very proud of you, top-1-A you'll be, you standing before us! I thank you, each and everyone of you. (Lummi Indian Doctor)

The young Salish Indian will find public recognition by "coming into *syə'wən* and dancing in front of the people". He cannot hope for direct material gain—unless his personal spirit power is so inclined—but he can hope for prestige among his peers who may say of him: "He's got a lot of friends, he's rich that way, in that organization he's valued high" (Y.I.). Even the most insignificant dancer will command respect when possessed by his spirit; he may conduct an orchestra of drummers, and when he (and his spirit) passes by in the dance, the audience will raise from their seats, clap hands and hum in the rhythm of his tune. Of each new dancer, the ritualist can justly proclaim:

Now everybody knows him, before nobody knew him.

Traditional concepts of the benefits of guardian spirit power (*vide* Duff 1952:97ff) are still held by modern spirit dance participants in the Upper Stalo region *in principle:* spirit powers afford the owner protection, good luck, and success in whatever life situation and task he wants to rely on them. They are generally credited with promoting his spiritual and physical well-being, sometimes (C.L.) also his material wealth. As can be gathered from the ritualists' warnings at ceremonials, spirit powers are understood to be easily offended by any neglect or infringement of the *syə'wən* rules. They react by withdrawal or by supernatural retaliation against the culprit and often also against his group. The collectivity, therefore, has a legitimate interest in preventing behaviour conflicting with *syə'wən* rules which all imply a personal responsibility towards one's group. Our data (*vide supra*, 75-79) suggest that guardian spirit power is seen as benefitting the responsible and harming the irresponsible owner, and as potentially affecting the collective in like manner. It follows, therefore, that anti-social uses of guardian spirit power (uses directed against the interests of the collective) are excluded in *syə'wən* theory.

The physical exercise and training the active spirit dancers go through from fall to spring every year is unparalleled by any amateur sport among the rest of the population. The degree of physical fitness and athletic proficiency achieved by some of the

Two famous healers: Professor Manfred Bleuler of Zurich, Switzerland, and Indian Doctor Isadore Tom of Lummi, Washington, 1976.

Salish shaman charm of bone. National Museum of Man.

Tzeachten ceremonial house, Sardis, B.C., 1976.

Interior of *Tzeachten* ceremonial house, Sardis, B.C., 1976.

Professor Claude Lévi-Strauss discussing Salish mythology with Chief Richard Malloway at author's home, 1974. (Photo: Jilek-Aall.)

Musqueam Elder Walker Stogan speaking at Indian Medicine Men's Panel, Canadian Psychiatric Association Transcultural Workshop, 1977.

Musqueam Elder Vincent Stogan with author at Seabird Island Indian Festival, 1976. (Photo: Jilek-Aall)

Kwakiutl Chief James Sewid, longterm friend of the author.

Author receiving Kwakiutl Indian name *Kas'lidi* ("The One Called Upon for Help"), Alert Bay, 1977.

Junior participants at Coast Salish festival.

Traditional welcome dance by Stalo Indian girls in shredded
bark costume.

Squamish and North Vancouver Indian dancers in full ceremonial attire. Dancer with cedar bark headdress.

Squamish Indian dancer with human hair headdress, 1971.

Chief Domanic Charlie, oldest dancer at Cultus Lake Indian
Festival 1968.

Squamish Chief Dan George with Salish Elders, 1968.

Lummi Indian dancers, 1967. Note headdresses of human hair and of feathers.

Stalo Indian dance group, 1971. The Point family. In foreground dancer with Coast Salish feather headdress.

Ernie Philip, renowned Shuswap Indian dancer, performing the
Eagle Dance at Cultus Lake Indian Festival, 1969.

Lummi Indian junior dancers accompanied by the drumming of
Elder Joe Washington, Lummi Indian Festival, 1971.

Lummi Indian spirit dancer with Coast Salish feather headdress. (Photo: Stern; see Ref. Stern, 1934)

Cowichan Indian spirit dancer with human hair headdress, 1912. (Photo: Curtis 1912; see Ref. Curtis 1913)

Young Salish Indian dancers.

Senior participants at Coast
Salish festival.

Traditional Indian *slahal* game, Indian Pow-wow, Mission City,
B.C., 1979.

Dr. Louise Jilek-Aall in conversation with the co-organizers of
Cultus Lake Indian Festivals, Chief and Mrs. Richard Malloway.

Coast Salish totem pole with *sxwaixwe* masks, Lummi, Washington.

Junior Indian dancers at Pow-wow, Mission City, B.C., 1979

Simon Baker, well known Salish elder.

sxwaixwe dance at namesgiving potlatch, Musqueam, B.C.

Chief Ben Paul leading *sxwaixwe* dancer, Musqueam, B.C., 1978.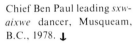

Coast Salish *sxwaixwe* mask on Stalo Indian rug 1970.

Construction of a Coast Salish dugout canoe.

Coast Salish Indian canoe racing.

Kwakiutl ceremonial house, Alert Bay, B.C. In front: Chief and
Mrs. James Sewid with Professor Bleuler.

Contemporary *skwəni'ləč̌* "twisted power stick", one of a pair made of naturally twisted cedar branches and bandaged with scarlet cloth; approx. size 25 x 40 cm. (Drawing by author, 1974)

Contemporary *skwəni'ləč̌* "power board" made of cedar, painted black on white; approx. size 30 x 45 cm. (Drawing by author, 1974)

Ancient Coast Salish spirit canoe ceremony: Shamans paddling to the land of the dead. (Photo: Leechman, taken at Tolt, Washington, July 12, 1920)

Ancient Coast Salish spirit canoe ceremony: Shamans returning from the land of the dead fight off pursuing ghosts who endanger spirit canoe. (Photo: Leechman, taken at Tolt, Washington, July 12, 1920)

Private collection Prof. E. Margetts, M.D.

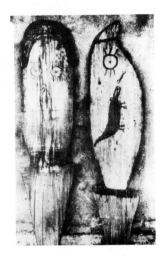

Spirit canoe planks with symbols of shamanic eye (above), "travellers", i.e. the shaman's spirit helpers (center), and dots representing the power songs revealed to the shaman. (Photo: Leechman, 1920)

Spirit canoe planks. Left: Two shamanic eyes. Right: Half fish-half otter spirit power. (Photo: Leechman, 1920)

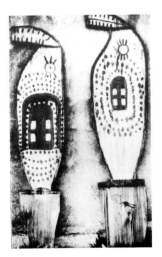

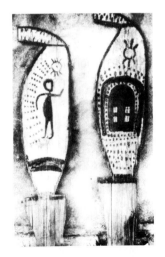

Spirit canoe planks with the symbols of *skudi'litc* spirit power (Photo: Leechman, 1920)

Spirit canoe planks. Left: Earth spirit with gestures of a dancing "sucking doctor". Right: *skudi'litc* spirit power with the "house of the cedar board people". (Photo: Leechman, 1920)

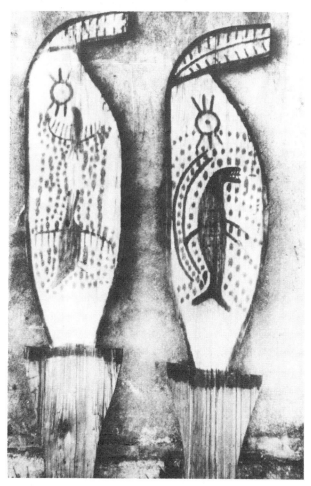

Spirit canoe planks, Left: Duck spirit powers swallowing illness, illness represented by short line between ducks. Right: *sxuda'tc* spirit power twisting victims into knots. (Photo: Leechman 1920)

(Private Collection Prof. E. Margetts, M.D.)

Restraining the *hamatsa* at Kwakiutl ceremonial, Cape Mudge, B.C., 1979.

Kwakiutl *hamatsa* ceremonial dance, Alert Bay, B.C., 1977.

Salish potlatch at Quamichan, Vancouver Island, 1913. Blankets being given away. (Photo supplied by W.A. Newcombe, Victoria, B.C., courtesy B.C. Provincial Archives)

sxwaixwe dance at Salish commemorative ceremony, Quamichan, 1900. (Photo supplied by W.A. Newcombe, Victoria, B.C., courtesy B.C. Provincial Archives)

sxwaixwe dancers at Salish funeral ceremony, Quamichan, 1910.
(Photo supplied by W.A. Newcombe, Victoria, B.C., courtesy
B.C. Provincial Archives)

Kwakiutl master carver Jimmy Dick directing "Animal Kingdom" dancers.

Kwakiutl "Animal Kingdom" ceremonial symbolizing harmony of man and nature. Alert Bay longhouse, 1972.

Cherokee master carver Lelooska directing Moon dancers at
Kwakiutl festivities, Cape Mudge, B.C., 1979.

Kwakiutl chiefs extending traditional welcome to guests arriving
for festivities at Cape Mudge, B.C., 1979.

Cowichan *sxwaixwe* dancer, 1912. (Photo: Curtis 1912; see Ref.
Curtis 1913)

Coast Salish *sxwaixwe* mask, 1912. (Photo: Curtis 1912; see Ref. Curtis, 1913)

Author's daughter admiring *K'san* Indian mask.

ered as serious correctional problems by law-enforcement agencies, one of them with a long record of confinements because of multi-delinquency and narcotic addiction.

One young patient who previously had not recovered when hospitalized for severe psychoneurotic-depressive symptoms, has been functioning without medical attention ever since initiation two years ago. We have already mentioned the case of a postmenopausal depression with numerous hospitalizations, improving after healing rites were performed on her during a winter dance ceremony.

The balance of evidence, anecdotal and preliminary as it may be by epidemiological standards, suggests that the indigenous therapeutic procedures of the spirit dance ceremonial are superior to Western methods, as far as Indian clientele is concerned, in the management of two symptom complexes:

1) conditions of ill health in which psychoneurotic and psychophysiologic mechanisms are prominent. These are the patients who figure in *syə'wən* lore as miraculous cures after having been "in and out of hospitals, given up by the doctors;"
2) antisocial and aggressive behaviour usually associated with alcohol or drug abuse, and emotionally or physically destructive to self and kin.

Different as these two syndromes may appear, psychotherapeutic contacts with Indian patients of either type has made us realize that *anomic depression* is often underlying both the intrapunitive and the aggressive responses which may alternate in some cases.

Indian ritualists, while acknowledging Western medicine to be effective in "ordinary", i.e. not spirit-connected diseases, consider native people with the above syndromes—albeit under labels different from those applied here—as candidates for spirit dance initiation. Clinical experience, too, would suggest that in these cases "Indian treatment" compares favourably with Western therapeutic or correctional approaches.

When looking at the "Indian alcohol problem",[1] the extent of which may be taken as epidemiologic indicator of the prevalence of anomic depression in the native population of North America, it must be admitted that orthodox Western medical and psychiatric treatment attempts have been rather ineffective and are as a rule limited to palliative crisis intervention. The influence of spirit

97

dance therapy on periodic excessive drinking—which, rather than clinical addiction to alcohol, is still the predominant pattern of alcohol abuse among Upper Stalo Indians—should therefore be of considerable interest to health and social scientists alike.

It may be mentioned first that many prominent participants in the ceremonial freely admit to heavy indulging in the past. This by no means detracts from their reputation in Indian communities, or from the reputation of spirit dancers as a group in which the most prestigious native families are represented. On the contrary, it credits the spirit of *syə'wən* with greater power than that inherent in the spirits of the White man's alcohol.[2] The rehabilitation of some hard drinkers may in popular opinion be attributed to the healing power of the ritualists:

> I know the Lummi outfit, they had men down there with real serious alcohol problems and they came out of it through dancing. I don't know what does it, whether the Indian Doctors give them something to hold it [alcohol] off them . . . There's supposed to be power in their [Indian Doctors'] minds, a lot of power. (L.T.)

The following general statements can be made concerning alcohol intake and spirit dance participation:
1) The leading ritualists and some prominent participants are total abstainers.
2) All but a few of the active "modern" spirit dancers in the Upper Stalo region abstain throughout ceremonial seasons.
3) All of the new dancers who completed their initiation in the Upper Stalo region have kept sobriety during the season of their initiation.
4) Inebriated persons are not permitted to attend ceremonials, even if they are not active dancers. This has a general discouraging effect on Indian drinking in the Upper Stalo region during winter time, as (a) intake of small amounts of liquor holds little attraction; (b) the major ceremonial occasions conflict with bigger drinking parties, both being customarily scheduled on weekends.
5) To several participants, the culture propaganda associated with the modern winter ceremonial *(vide infra)*, suggests an active involvement in off-season native enterprises, such as Indian

98

festivals, canoe races and other Indian sports which require them to stay sober during training periods in summer months.

6) However, the rank and file of participants, including the majority of the spirit dancers, continue to consume liquor outside the ceremonial season. Most "modern" dancers apparently feel free to do so after their first year in *syə'wən* is over, although they are generally credited with having reduced their intake as compared to preinitiation times. Those spirit dancers who are also staunch members of Indian Alcoholics Anonymous groups remain abstinent. Some senior participants, therefore, recommend adherence to Alcoholics Anonymous during summer in addition to active participation in the winter ceremonial, for those with serious alcohol problems.

One may ask whether the ceremonial has failed in its postulated therapeutic functions if some participants return to drinking and drug abuse. Rehabilitation of alcoholics and drug addicts is only one band in the broad therapeutic spectrum of the spirit ceremonial, albeit one of great importance to the health and welfare of the Coast Salish people. Not enough time has elapsed to statistically demonstrate the effectiveness of the spirit dance ceremonial in achieving a *lasting* rehabilitation of initiates with serious alcohol and drug problems. However, it is fair to remember that many members of Alcoholics Anonymous "fall off the wagon", i.e. resume drinking, yet nobody today questions the general therapeutic effectiveness of Alcoholics Anonymous in combating alcoholism. The fact that the spirit ceremonial for at least five months every year provides most active dancers with sobriety and reduces the risk of alcohol abuse in many other participants, ranks it with the major therapies of alcoholism. It can be said that, with the possible exceptions of Alcoholics Anonymous and the Indian Shaker Church, nothing of equal therapeutic efficacy has ever been undertaken to fight the Indian alcohol problem in the Coast Salish area.

Footnotes

1. The extent of this problem in North America is discussed in a report of the Indian Health Service Task Force on Alcoholism (1969) which concludes that "alcoholism is one of the most serious health problems facing the Indian people today". Regarding the reflection of this problem in British Columbia vital statistics, see Schmitt et al. (1966). The association of alcohol and drug abuse with mortality due to accident and violence is generally acknowledged for North American populations. Among the major causes of death in registered Indians of British Columbia in 1972, death due to accident, poisoning and violence ranked prominent in the age groups 7-16 years (84.2% of all deaths) and 17-40 (66.6%). Suicide and drug overdosage accounted for 28.8% of the accidental deaths from age 17 to 60 years (The Indian Voice, February 1974:12).

2. Salish Indians had no alcoholic beverages in pre-contact times.

Chapter Eight

From Psychohygienic Ritual to Ritual Psychotherapy

At this point it will be appropriate to draw some generalizing conclusions from ethnographic data and our own observations in an effort to delineate the main psychosocial functions of the Salish guardian spirit ceremonial, both in the past and present. In traditional Coast Salish culture, the *spirit quest* had a prominent place in the ceremonial complex and was the main path toward acquisition of power and full participation in the ritual.

As for the importance of the spirit quest for personality development, we can rely on the assessment of an authority like Driver who asserts that:

> In the process of acquiring the many markers of maturity, no experience was as important as the acquisition of a spirit-helper in a vision quest . . . without it, a man would fail in all important undertakings, such as hunting, warfare, and curing the sick.

> The function of the vision in education was to instill confidence in a young person so that he would attempt things considered impossible before such a religious experience. With a spirit helper at his beck and call, an insecure adolescent would become more self-sufficient and would take more initiative in such necessary activities as war and the chase. (Driver 1969:391-392)

The quest for, and the acquisition of, spirit helpers had to be completed in adolescence or young adulthood. It is at this stage that the young individual has to achieve a sense of sexual and sociocultural identity from which feelings of emotional security and social belonging can be derived. When returning from his successful spirit quest at the age of fourteen years, Old Pierre felt sure that he was going to be a real man, a true Katzie Indian, and a great medicine-man. As Erikson (1950) has formulated, and as many a life history shows, the danger of this developmental stage lies in role confusion with its psychopathological and sociopathological consequences. Confusion about their social and cultural role, and the "inability to settle on an occupational identity" (Erikson 1950) are major disturbing factors in the personality development of young people in modern Western societies. "In their search for a new sense of continuity and sameness, adolescents . . . are ever ready to install lasting idols and ideals as *guardians of a final identity.*" (Erikson 1950:261; italics mine) This was precisely the tutelary spirit's role in Salish culture; namely, to act as guardian of the young Indian's final identity and thus to ward off the frustration and depression which accompanies role confusion. The altered state of consciousness of the vision experience was striven after only as means to attain a spirit helper; it was not an end in itself.

The Indian youth's quest for a guardian spirit, therefore, was a quest for his identity and meaning[1] in life.

As we have seen, the traditional Salish spirit quest involved conditions and techniques suitable for the induction of altered states of consciousness, and the spirit encounter typically took place in such a state. Spirit dance initiation, with techniques analogous to those of the vision-quest, later recreated this altered state of consciousness, repeating the previous learning experience of the adolescent spirit quest. This experience thereafter facilitated the new dancer's re-entering into ritual trances so that he could display his spirit power or powers, which were always seen as enhancing the dancer's welfare and preventing or alleviating physical, emotional, and social distress.

In more recent ethnographic reports, we see the spirit quest receding in importance behind the initiation. In Upper Stalo culture (*vide* Duff 1952:97; 102ff) guardian spirit power was never conceived of as innate in the individual, nor was it held to be inheritable. It had to be acquired through spirit quest, or was bestowed by the guardian spirit upon the individual in an altered state of consciousness, without previous quest. "Dancer's power" could also be instilled through actions of old dancers (Duff, *op. cit.:*105), but according to information we obtained from the most prominent senior dancer in the region, such procedures were very rarely resorted to in the era of traditional spirit dancing. Today, the spirit dance initiation is the main delivery system of

102

spirit power to candidates, while in the past it was understood as a test or confirmation of power previously obtained elsewhere from supernaturals through individual efforts or as a "gift". This change in the ceremonial is frequently commented upon by senior participants, for example:

In the older days you got your song from the woods, in the forest; the power seemed to come natural to them, without anybody working on them . . . Then they tested it if you really got it, you had to prove it [in the initiation]; if you could do it, they accepted you. (C.L.)

Now instead of the young man going out and looking for his spirit in the woods, we can no longer do that because the places they went are no longer free—so now we only have the initiation. (L.S.)

Some formal alterations of the traditional ceremonial, such as the predominant use of English in lieu of Salish tongues in ritual speech making, or the disappearance of texts from the spirit dance songs, appear of lesser importance than this fading away of a separate spirit quest. However, it must not be overlooked that guardian spirit acquisition has become a most essential feature of the initiation process itself.

Another significant change is that spirit illness, in the old culture a strictly seasonal, stereotyped pathomorphic goal-directed state inevitably leading to spirit singing and dancing, is now in many cases the traditional label for the depressive syndrome associated with experiences of relative deprivation and identity confusion which we have called anomic depression. This condition has a tendency towards chronicity, and is in many cases not restricted to a brief seasonal course. It is essentially a depressive reaction with sufficient patho-plastic cultural coloring of its symptoms to permit identification as spirit illness and provide an indication for treatment by spirit dance initiation. Our data bear out that this depression-anxiety syndrome is recognized by the ritualists and by those concerned about the patient, as an indication for sya'wən therapy. Moreover, clinical experience suggests that Indian patients who outwardly show disruptive behaviour associated with alcohol or drug absue, are often basically de-

103

pressed. We can, therefore, assume that anomic depression in its various manifestations is today a major factor in bringing young Indians into *syə'wən*. While the model for the therapeutic role of spirit dance initiation was provided by traditional culture (obligatory cure of all spirit illness), initiation was in the past not conceived of primarily as a healing procedure, rather as a necessary test of the personally acquired spirit powers the candidates wanted to display in their dances. Senior participants agree that "torturing to bring out the song" was not necessary and was not a general practice in bygone days. It seems plausible that procedures in the service of personality depatterning have to be made more efficient now in order to pave the way for the reorientation of emotionally and socially maladjusted candidates towards the ideal norms of Indian culture as conceptualized by the leaders. The task of initiation is no longer only to provide entrance into a ceremonial, *via* the cure of a ritualized pathomorphic state, through rebirth as a new human being, but to overcome sickness and faulty behaviour contracted by exposure to an alien culture, through rebirth as a true Indian. This is the ritualists' message at the namesgiving ceremony—today part of the initiation process—in which the revival of ancestral names is solemnly proclaimed and witnessed:

> You have a new life as an Indian now! (Rosedale, Dec. 12, 1970)

> He remembered his grandmother's Indian name, he wants his granddaughter to carry this Indian name. All of you that were called as witnesses tonight: this young lady will be known as S., this was the grandmother of this friend of ours. This name will come back to life and it's going to be carried by this young girl . . .

> When it comes to *syə'wən* like this, the parents start to think back. The father of this boy is going to bring back the name of his great-great-grandfather: O. His name is coming back to be known and carried by this young man . . . this name has become alive once more, this name is something that you will be proud of because if comes from our ancestors! (Tzeachten, February 19, 1971)

> Last weekend Tzeachten was invited to LaConner and

104

there was this young man receiving his Indian name. His father wanted this Indian name remembered in Chilliwack, so tonight this boy is here fulfilling the wish of his ancestors. Those who are called as witnesses, we ask you to remember the name in the language of our people! (Tzeachten, February 27, 1971)

Through spirit dance initiation the young native, estranged from his traditional culture as he may be, not only acquires his *Indian Power;* in the namesgiving ceremony an ancestral name comes to life again and with it the insignia of an *Indian identity* are bestowed on the new dancer—he has been reborn as an Indian and has made the crucial step in his quest for identity and meaning in life.

In the past, the length of *syə'wən* season was rigidly fixed according to region, and dancing out of season was highly exceptional[2]—it was also unnecessary, as everybody's urge to dance ended with the ceremonial season. If we assume modern spirit dancing to fill genuine therapeutic needs in genuinely pathological conditions, then we should find the duration of what we described as annual winter therapy adjusted to individual needs. This is exactly what now happens in the Upper Stalo region: some dancers continue to practice long after the official end of the season, or resume "singing" in early fall, assisted by friends who drum for them privately.

With the near extinction of other forms of native healing, the winter spirit ceremonial has become the only major non-Western therapy at the disposal of the Coast Salish Indians. Its therapeutic scope has been widened by integrating a new shamanic curing rite *(skʷəni'ləx́)*,[4] by more extensive use of depatterning and reconditioning procedures in the initiation process; and also by a new focus on those Indian patients for whom Western medicine has little to offer.

From the data reviewed and presented in the foregoing chapters, we conclude that what in the past was a ritual with psychohygienic aspects is now an organized Indian effort at culture-congenial psychotherapy.

Recently, Amoss (1972) has presented her findings in a doctoral dissertation on the persistence of aboriginal traditions among the Nooksack, which amounts to a modern ethnography of this

Coast Salish population in the border region of Northwestern Washington.[3] In her work, Amoss gives a detailed description of the "Indian way" beliefs and practices among the Nooksack which correspond to those of their Coast Salish neighbours with whom they maintain close ceremonial ties (cf. Suttles 1963). The "ceremonies of the Indian way", as Amoss calls them, centre around the winter dancing complex. However, observances of the previously separate "ghost complex" such as memorials for the dead, and the main elements of the secular potlatch festival have become integrated in the winter ceremonial. They constitute what is commonly referred to in Salish smokehouses as the "work". Amoss' definition of the three essential elements of Nooksack winter dance gatherings—(1) hospitality, shown in the generous reception and feeding of guests, (2) spirit dancing proper, (3) "work" with public announcements of status changes and meeting of obligations,—is valid also for the contemporary winter ceremonial life of the Stalo, Musqueam and Lummi Indians. The same can be said of the *functions of spirit dancing*, which Amoss discerns among the Nooksack. In summarized form, Amoss (*op. cit:* 187) lists the following manifest functions (i.e., professed by the actors) of spirit dancing: On the social level, it keeps the group together and socializes deviants; on the cultural level it preserves the heritage; on the individual level it preserves health and provides opportunity for recreation and social interaction. Latent functions of the ceremonial (i.e. deduced by the observer) are: On the social level, it encourages investment in the ceremonial system, ramifies and intensifies intertribal ties and promotes group solidarity; on the cultural level, it expresses essential cultural values and reconciles contradictions between them; on the individual level, it allows expression of spontaneity and creativity, provides personal recognition, and affirms Indian identity and group belonging.

While these are clearly discernible functions of contemporary Salish winter ceremonials, in which spirit dancing proper has been combined with other traditional ceremonies, both sacred and profane, it is nevertheless true that all these functions also serve a therapeutic purpose as they ultimately promote the alleviation of anxiety and the maximization of a feeling of well-being and security in the individual and the collective. Amoss (*op.cit.*:188) herself observes that "the therapeutic function is of overwhelm-

106

ing importance to the Indians themselves." Even the seemingly unfavourable economic consequences of the ceremonial system which Amoss (*op.cit.*:207) sees as draining off the surpluses of cash, time and energy and thereby tending to "perpetuate the proverty of the entire Indian community", have the effect of preventing the Indians from full participation in the North American economic system and thus "provide one of the factors which prevent them from assimilating to the dominant society." (*op.cit.*:200)

It would be naive to assume that in the absence of a sacred winter ceremonial the love of festivity and group hospitality,—so deeply ingrained in Coast Salish cultures and also attested to by Amoss' ethnographic data—would not find more profane outlets, albeit less salubrious due to the then inevitable liquor consumption, but certainly not less costly than spirit dancing.

More important appears the issue of assimilation. Quite apart from its feasibility,—the dominant society in North America has so far proven incapable of truly assimilating any of the substantial non-Caucasian minority groups, rather they tend to be tucked away in urban slums under conditions of economic exploitation and racial discrimination,—the question arises, whether assimilation is a desirable goal even for the individual Indian. Judging from historical experiences we shall have to concede that attempts at assimilation of Indian populations have resulted in deculturation rather than acculturation. Attempts at luring Indian people away from their cultural identity by the offer of economic baits and under the pretext of a phony egalitarianism, have led to the deleterious psychosocial consequences of *anomie*. The kind of participation in the economic system of the dominant society that is in store for deculturated Indians in North America can be observed on the skid rows of Western cities. We agree with Amoss (*op.cit.*:208) that "the greatest social benefit of the ceremonial system is . . . the preservation of the Indian group against the threat of assimilation". However, we would argue, on the basis of the clinical data presented in chapter four, that the preservation of a distinct Indian identity has survival value not only for the group but also for the individual, as it forestalls the ultimately self-destructive process of *anomic depression.*

Footnotes

1. "Meaning" in the sense used by Frankl (1963) as "logos" or "meaning of human existence".

2. According to senior dancers who frown upon such irregularity.

3. I am grateful to W. Suttles for drawing my attention to Amoss' work which became available after the present manuscript was essentially completed.

4. It appears that the $sk^w\partial ni'l\partial\check{c}$ ceremony as practiced today, and its paraphernalia, derive from the ancient shamanistic voyage to the Land of the Dead for the purpose of curing a patient by recovering his guardian spirit or his soul which had been abducted by ghosts. The dangerous trip was the theme of an elaborate pantomimic psychodrama performed in winter before large audiences by powerful shamans who travelled for several nights in a magical "spirit-canoe" over land and rivers to the underworld and back. This was the $sbEtEtda'q$ ceremony described by Haeberlin (1918). It was first recorded among the southern Coast Salish by M. Eells (Smithsonian Institution Annual Report 1887:605-681, Washington 1889) and G. A. Dorsey (Bulletin of the Free Museum of Science and Art of the University of Pennsylvania 3:227-238;1902), and also mentioned by Curtis (1913:110). Later it was analysed in detail by T. T. Waterman (Indian Notes, Museum of the American Indian, Heye Foundation, 7:129-148;295-312;535-561, New York 1930).

Chapter Nine

Modern Spirit Dancing
as a Therapeutic Social Movement

In an attempt to define and localize modern Salish spirit dancing as a social phenomenon, general analyses of cultural and religious movements were reviewed. In this task the student is assisted by the work of Aberle (1966:315-333) who not only provides the relevant references, but also a comprehensive classification of social movements. Aberle defines a social movement as "an organized effort by a group of human beings to effect change in the face of resistance by other human beings", and classifies such movements according to the dimensions of locus and amount of change they aim at, as

1) *transformative:* total change in supra-individual systems (in the context of therapy: cure of collectives);[1]
2) *reformative:* partial change in supra-individual systems (improvement of collectives);
3) *redemptive:* total change in individuals (cure of individuals);
4) *alterative:* partial change in individuals (improvement of individuals).

These are, of course, analytical categories, and componential elements of one type of movement may be found in others. What Aberle stresses as more important, however, is that "any given movement may change in type over time". We might, therefore, see a redemptive movement reaching beyond its original aim of effecting a cure of the individual and work towards curing the socio-cultural system. In fact, as Aberle points out, "virtually all redemptive movements, like the transformative movements, reject at least some features of the current society." Basically, however, the "defining characteristic" of redemptive movements "is the search for a new inner state" and their common doctrine is that "changes in behaviour can result only from a new state of grace". Constant features of redemptive movements are organized efforts (1) to overcome the individual's resistant or apathetic attitude *vis-à-vis* the desirable change; (2) to increase the in-group contacts

109

and/or decrease the out-group contacts of participants.

The reader who has followed our description of the resurgence, growth, and current practice of the winter ceremonial in the Upper Stalo region, will recognize the applicability of Aberle's characterization of redemptive movements to contemporary Salish spirit dancing: An organized effort by ritualists, active dancers and other believers in *syə'wən*, to effect a total personality change, a "rebirth" in individuals whose apathy or resistance to this change has to be overcome by the depatterning and re-orientation procedures of the initiation process; further, an attempt at sheltering the candidates from out-group influences, and at safeguarding their loyalty and future participation through appropriate indoctrination and organizational arrangements, buttressed by social and supernatural sanctions.

We have earlier referred to Aberle's concept of relative deprivation in the context of contemporary spirit illness. Through our contacts with local Indians we have obtained the impression that the majority of native Canadians in the Upper Stalo region feel they suffer relative deprivation in the areas of possessions, status, behaviour, and worth; in evaluating their situation, they use the dominant White Canadian society as their "reference field".[2] However, when gauging Indian consciousness of relative deprivation we found this most pronounced in the statements of the active propagandists of the spirit dance movement. This is in line with Aberle's assumption that relative deprivation is "the seedbed for social movements". While realizing that modern Salish spirit dancing does not qualify as a transformative movement, we may draw attention to the presence in the modern spirit dance movement of important tendencies no longer aiming merely at the "rebirth" of individual Indians, but at a *collective Indian renaissance*. These tendencies are associated with ideological concepts implying radical changes in the goal-orientation of native groups and in the relationship between native and dominant society. Such "renaissant" trends were not active in the traditional ceremonial, but are gaining momentum since it has been revived in the Upper Stalo region. Partisans of the modern spirit dance movement refer to "membership in *syə'wən*", and to the creation of a "bigger social family for all Salish tribes" through *syə'wən*; they believe that the "revival of Indian customs and traditions" is the answer to many Indian problems, and they feel

110

an obligation to "work together to revive the Old Indian ways" and to "teach the young Indian that the Indian Way does have a meaning". There can indeed be no doubt about the significance of the spirit dance movement for the development of a national consciousness in the "Salish Nation"—a term often heard now at ceremonial gatherings in the Fraser Valley. Conscious efforts are made by Indian leaders to revive the Salish heritage and to uphold to the young native generation the exemplary ideal of *Indianness*, a Pan-Indian rallying sign akin to the Pan-African *négritude* of Césaire and Senghor. In their espousal of Indianness, spokesmen at spirit dance ceremonials follow the example of outstanding Indian figures like George Clutesi or Chief Dan George, who confront Indian and White audiences with an idealized image of aboriginal culture, juxtapositional to the obvious defects of Western civilization,[3] in this way creating what Schwimmer (1970) has termed an *opposition ideology*. This ideology contrasts the "spiritual" and altruistic orientation of Indian culture with the "egoistic materialism" prevailing in Western civilization.

Not long after the revival of spirit dancing in the region, a reporter of the local newspaper was told by active supporters of the ceremonial:

> Ingrained into the nature of an Indian person is the idea that living is for giving. We always took only what was needed. We preserved food for winter together. Everyone was his brother's keeper . . . an Indian house is never too small to take in another person, or even another family . . . the wealthy man was the man who could give most. In white society, the wealthy man is the one who can keep the most for himself. This is where our cultures conflict." (The Chilliwack Progress, July 8, 1970:3B)

As the knowledge of Salishan languages is on the wane among the younger Indian generations, adherence to a "spiritual life" according to the "Old Indian Ways" has become the hallmark of Indianness. In the Upper Stalo region, to display an active interest in the winter ceremonial today means to profess one's Indian identity, and also one's belief in the rebirth of Indian culture and in the future of the Salish nation. What may be called *culture propaganda* has a definite place in the modern spirit ceremonial.

111

Thus is the ritualists' message to the people:

> The Salish nation has a lot to be proud of; let us be proud of our Indian ways! (Rosedale, Dec. 12, 1970)

> This is our way, the Indian way. This is the way of our ancestors. Only by being proud of it can we stay Indian. We Indians are not looking for material goods, we look for a free life. We don't seek material things, we seek spiritual power! (Seabird Island, Jan. 12, 1970)

> Our Indian culture is not dead, it is alive today, our ancestors feel happy about what they see. When I was young, when the old people died the fires burnt down and the old smokehouses fell down, so keep the fires burning again! Everything changes, *syə'wən* changes, too, but I know you'll keep the fires burning . . . There is every reason you should be proud of your Indian culture. As long as the sun rises in the East and sets in the West, and as long as the streams go to the ocean these fires will burn. (Tzeachten, Jan. 8, 1971)

> Your great-great-grandparents have started the fires to burn in these smokehouses in bygone days. You carry the heritage of your ancestors. These Indians names, the names of a great people, these names were known throughout the land and they will be known again! Nowadays we are all related in one way or another, this is why the words come out, because our Indian people all belong together. Those in *syə'wən* here turn around to teach the young that's coming behind; without that our Indian ways would all be forgotten . . . Help one another at all times so that the Indian ways will grow! (Tzeachten, Feb. 19. 1971)

The promoters of the spirit dance movement stress its appeal to all Indians living in the area. While only a selected group—"those who need it"—are expected to become active dancers, the leaders' *culture propaganda* aims at a broad Indian participation by mass attendance and involvement of many native people in tasks connected with the ceremonial. On the other hand, some of the younger spirit dancers militate for the elimination of whatever

112

they perceive as "White" influence and interference. The most radical among them are against any sort of cooperation even with sympathetic "White" therapeutic and social agencies; they discourage Indian clientage of such agencies and demand the exclusion of all White guests from the ceremonial.[4] Here the voice of a young radical:

No White man can help an Indian, no White man really wants to help an Indian. The Indians who don't know what's there for them [in spirit dancing] are stupid, because that's the only thing that can help them, if they come back to their own culture. No White man can help an Indian, only Indians can do that. I had to find that out, only Indians can help an Indian, White people only get them into trouble. (N.A.)

All these strivings, which go beyond the goals usually set in a therapeutic enterprise, reveal a keynote of *nativism*, i.e., an attitude of systematic favouring of the cultural in-group as opposed to the cultural out-group. (cf. Ames 1957) Specific characteristics of social movements with nativistic orientation can be identified in the development of spirit dancing in the Upper Stalo region:
1) characteristics of a *revivalistic-nativistic movement*, (Linton 1943), namely a "conscious, organized attempt on the part of a society's members to revive . . . selected aspects of its culture", in a "situation of inequality between the societies in contact";
2) characteristics of a *revitalization movement* (Wallace 1956), namely a "deliberate, organized, conscious effort by members of a society to construct a more satisfying culture", in type both *nativistic* ("elimination of alien persons, customs, values") and *revivalistic* ("institution of customs, values, and even aspects of nature which are thought to have been in the mazeway of previous generations but are not now present");
3) characteristics of a *resistive nativistic movement* (Ames 1957) with "resistance to the beliefs, values, and practices of the dominant society".
These pertinent characterizations can be included in a classificatory schema of the spirit dance movement, a schema which combines the typologies of Aberle (op. cit.:316) and Clemhout

113

(1964:14), and which is intended to provide clues for predicting potential future developments. In considering future developments one may be reminded that the living-space of the Salishan speaking peoples has in the nineteenth century been the arena of an important religious movement, the Prophet Dance;[5] from which originated the (transformative) Ghost Dance,[6] a series of often militantly anti-White movements of "sacro-nativistic" type sweeping through native North America. It is as yet unclear whether a secularized analogy will be provided in our time by transformative revitalization movements of "politico-nativistic" type, inspired by the so-called "Red Power" ideology, which appeals to some of the younger spirit dancers.

The Coast Salish area has in the past also seen the rise of Shakerism,[7] a redemptive movement of the "sacro-syncretic" type in which shamanic practices, guardian-spirit beliefs, catholic liturgy and protestant ethic blended to form a religious cult, eventually established as a church. Developments in such a direction would require a deliberate amalgamation of contemporary *syə'wən* doctrines with trends in modern Western Zeitgeist which already exercise a significant yet concealed influence on Indian thought, into a sacro-syncretic belief system, or into an ethico-syncretic ideology. In the post-imperialist era, ideological currents in contemporary Western societies suggest the abandonment of eurocentric, positivistic and "materialistic" world-views, concomitant with an upgrading, even idealization, of the Western image of non-Western cultures. These currents are reflected in a changing Indian-White relationship and may eventually effect the merging of the Indian "opposition ideology" with that of the younger White generation.

Footnotes

1. All references to therapy added by present author.

2. Cf. Aberle *op. cit.*:324.

3. Cf., for example: Dr. Clutesi's convocation address at the University of Victoria, May 1971; and Chief Dan George's address at a recent dinner meeting. (The Indian Voice, March 1972:13)

114

4. A few Whites are invited by their Indian friends to attend as guests. There are also a couple of Caucasian spirit dancers from Washington State who are related to Indians and live in Indian communities (reverse acculturation). Recent anti-White sentiment among young radicals tends to differentiate on a racial rather than on a cultural or ideological basis.

5. Cf. Spier's (1935) research on the Prophet Dance and the origin of the Ghost Dance; also Suttles (1957); both authors have specific references to the Prophet Dance in the Upper Stalo region, but do not examine the relationship between Prophet Dance and spirit dancing.

6. Cf. Du Bois (1939) for the Ghost Dance of the 1870s; for the later movements around 1890 see the classical treatise by Mooney (1896). Guariglia (1959:149-171; 190-193) provides a comprehensive review with geographical maps.

7. Cf. Gunther (1949), Collins (1950), and above all, Barnett (1957).

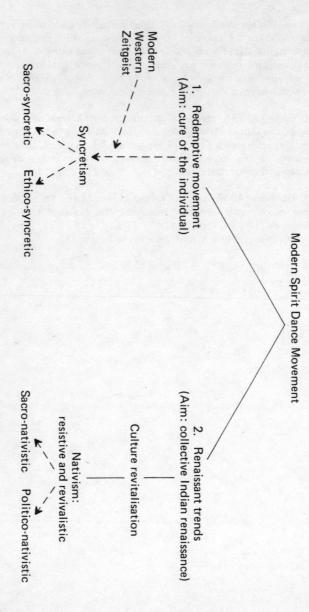

Modern Spirit Dance Movement

1. Redemptive movement
(Aim: cure of the individual)

Modern
Western
Zeitgeist

Syncretism

Sacro-syncretic

Ethico-syncretic

2. Renaissant trends
(Aim: collective Indian renaissance)

Culture revitalisation

Nativism:
resistive and revivalistic

Sacro-nativistic

Politico-nativistic

116

Chapter Ten
Anomic Depression: Why Indian People Die

In the fifty years between 1924 and 1974, the population of
Canada increased 2.5 times, and the population of British
Columbia increased 4.4 times, mainly as a result of immigration. In these fifty years, the statutory registered Indian
population of Canada increased 2.6 times and that of British
Columbia increased 2.1 times—without immigration. In 1973,
1.2% of all Canadians and 2.2% of all British Columbians were
statutory registered Indians. The registered "status" Indian
population of British Columbia has risen from 50,973 in 1973
to 55,611 in 1979.[1] Much higher is the total number of native
peoples—those who have status under the *Indian Act* plus those
who are "non-status" Indians because of marriage to non-
Indians or because of other legal processes of "enfranchise-
ment". However, there are no official statistics on racial "non-
status" Indians, because the recording of ethnicity or race is
discouraged by the government—an egalitarian rule which
serves politicians rather than ethnic groups with special needs.

In this growing native population, administered to by the
Indian Act, the leading causes of death are accident and
violence, as documented in the *Vital Statistics Annual Reports
of British Columbia*, 1963 to 1979. In the fifteen-year period
from 1965 to 1979, the British Columbia Indian rates for death
from accident have on average been three times higher than
those of the total population of the province; the Indian rates
for death from suicide were nearly double; and the Indian
homicide victim rates averaged more than eight times those of
the total population. Death from alcohol-induced cirrhosis of
the liver occurred on average nearly three times as often in the
registered Indian as in the total population of British Columbia.
Due to the above mentioned peculiarities of statistical recording
in Canada, vital statistics cannot compare racial Indians with
non-Indians, but only registered Indians with the entire
provincial population, which already includes the native
people and their elevated death rates.

117

Since 1977, the federal medical services, Pacific region, have submitted annual reports with detailed morbidity and mortality data on British Columbia Indians which reveal a sombre picture.[2] Accidents, poisoning and violence caused 37% of all British Columbia Indian deaths in 1977, 36% in 1978, and again 37% in 1979. Of particular concern is the preponderance of death due to accidents and violence in the younger age groups. In the 1-4 years age group, 71% (1977), 53% (1978), and 67% (1979) of all deaths were due to accidents or violence; in the 5-14 years age group the respective figures were 86% (1977), 64% (1978), 56% (1979), and in the 15-29 years age group 83% (1977), 85% (1978), and 84% (1979). The role of alcohol in producing these high rates has been ascertained. In 1978, 39% of all deaths among British Columbia Indians were attributable to alcohol, while an estimated 80% of all accidental and violent deaths of British Columbia Indians throughout recent years were associated with alcohol abuse. Indian deaths recorded as due to "mental disorder" are on close inspection invariably revealed to be related to alcohol abuse and its sequelae. The relatively high rates of death due to "digestive diseases" in British Columbia Indians are also explained by alcoholism, as alcohol-induced liver cirrhosis accounted for 60% of such deaths in 1977, 69% in 1978 and 63% in 1979.

The British Columbia Indian suicide rate has been of particular concern to the federal medical services of the Pacific region. Information gathered by their staff and by the native Community Health Representatives illuminates the real tragedy behind the overall suidice rates—namely their age distribution. The great majority of native suicides occur in the 15-29 years age group; 62% of all suicides by British Columbia Indians in 1977, 81% in 1978 and 75% in 1979 occurred in this group.

118

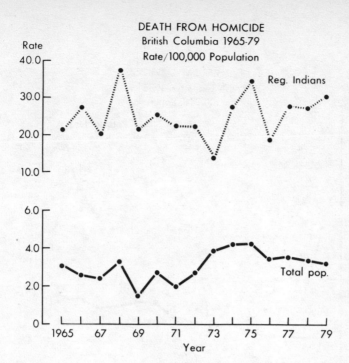

DEATH FROM HOMICIDE
British Columbia 1965-79
Rate/100,000 Population

Reg. Indians

Total pop.

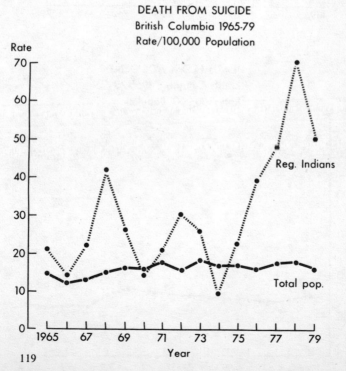

DEATH FROM SUICIDE
British Columbia 1965-79
Rate/100,000 Population

Reg. Indians

Total pop.

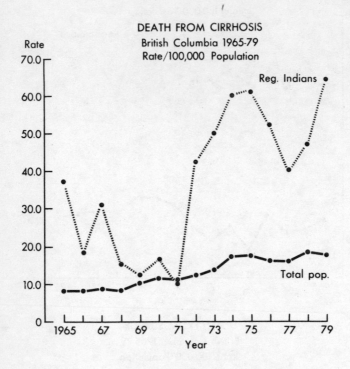

DEATH FROM CIRRHOSIS
British Columbia 1965-79
Rate/100,000 Population

Reg. Indians

Total pop.

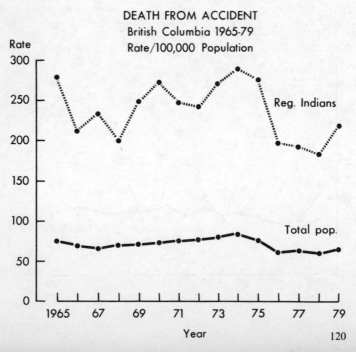

DEATH FROM ACCIDENT
British Columbia 1965-79
Rate/100,000 Population

Reg. Indians

Total pop.

Analogous suicide patterns have been found in other North American Indian populations (cf. overviews by May and Dizmang 1974; Willard 1979).

The psychiatrist dealing with self-damaging young native persons finds them to be in a double identity crisis—both the general personal identity crisis of youth and the specific cultural identity crisis of Indian youth. Today a young native person is often alienated from his cultural traditions and cannot feel pride and respect for his people, nor can he identify with the culture and tradition of the majority society. A helpless drifter between two worlds, he may see in a quasi-heroic suicidal act the only opportunity of exercising mastery over his destiny.

> One life and one life lone and life so mix-up... I will not die as a coward to face life, but to live in the land of my forefathers. To die as a man. To show no fear. (Suicide note of an Indian teenage boy).

Information gathered by native Community Health Representatives and tabulated in the *Medical Services Annual Reports* reveal the following factors as consistently and immediately operant in suicidal acts of young British Columbia Indians.

(1) *Social factors*
   (a) Personal isolation (absence of close interpersonal ties; experience of loss of significant persons; interpersonal discord).
   (b) Disturbed family support network (lack or loss of stable home environment; disrupted family situation).
(2) *Emotional factors*
   Prevailing mood of dysphoria (feeling depressed and unhappy).
(3) *Toxic factors*
   History of alcohol and/or drug abuse (often suicidal action while under toxic influence).
(4) *Seasonal factors*
   Predilection for fall and winter months (especially October, November, December).[3]

121

Similar psychosocial and toxic factors were found to be associated with native homicide in a study comparing killings committed by Canadian Indians and non-Indians (Jilek and Roy 1976). In this investigation, conducted in federal penal institutions in British Columbia, Canadian Indian homiciders were found to be different from White Anglo-Canadian homiciders on several parameters, prominent among which were the lack of purposefulness of the homicidal act and the predominant association of homicide and previous delinquency with alcohol abuse. Lack of exposure to traditional Indian culture was associated with early age onset of asocial and delinquent behaviour and lower age at first homicide. There was a history of alcohol-connected psychosocial problems in every Indian case, but no evidence of endogenous psychosis, sexual deviancy or perversion could be elicited, while such was not uncommon among White homiciders. The great majority of homicidal acts committed by Indian offenders consisted in senseless slaying of kin or close band members, and would therefore have been absolutely unacceptable in pre-contact aboriginal cultures. Hence these acts cannot be explained by recourse to any factors inherent in native culture. Rather, the exceedingly high rate of native homicide victims, killed for the most part by relatively young kin or neighbours in senseless acts without any logical criminal objective, reveals the degree of *de*culturation which has taken place among the younger native generation. The role of alcohol—the toxic agent introduced and sometimes imposed by Whites—in breaking down the fabric of Indian societies, and the changing patterns of Indian liquor consumption from ceremonial *potlatch*-type feast drinking to habitual intake in order to escape from painful reality, has recently been examined for the coastal Indian population of British Columbia by Jilek-Aall (1974, 1978). She saw in the formation of native Alcoholics Anonymous groups with emphasis on traditional values a culture-congenial response to threatening native self-destruction.

The prominent place occupied by alcoholism among the

problems affecting homes on Indian reserves was documented in a community survey conducted by native health workers in three representative Indian communities of the British Columbia coast area.[4] In her report, the research coordinator emphasized that alcoholism was included as a problem only if it reached severe proportions and had a marked effect on others living in the same home. In a small, isolated, and remote reserve, accessible only by boat or plane, the ranking of problems affecting the fourteen households of the community were:

Alcoholism	9 (64% of all households)
Marital breakdown	6 (43% of all households)
Welfare problems	4 (29% of all households)
Violence	1 (7% of all households)
Financial problems	1 (7% of all households)
No significant problems	2 (14% of all households)

In a rural reserve relatively close to, but not integrated into, a population centre, the problems affecting the 58 households were:

Alcoholism	38 (66% of all households)
Welfare problems	22 (38% of all households)
Marital breakdown	14 (24% of all households)
Overcrowded home	13 (22% of all households)
Child neglect	6 (10% of all households)
Violence	1 (2% of all households)
No significant problems	10 (17% of all households)

In an Indian reserve bordering on a city, the following problems affected the 55 households:

Alcoholism	18 (33% of all households)
Welfare problems	12 (22% of all households)
Marital breakdown	10 (18% of all households)
Violence	7 (13% of all households)
Financial problems	3 (5% of all households)
No significant problems	8 (15% of all households)

A comparative study of case records of patients seen by Dr. Jilek-Aall and myself through the years 1966 to 1974 in British Columbia (Jilek-Aall, Jilek and Flynn 1978) revealed significant associations between psychopathology and cultural background. For most patients who belonged to three well-defined ethnic cultural groups (Coast Salish Indians, Russian Doukhobors, and Germanic Mennonites) it was possible to correctly predict their membership in either group solely on the basis of the recorded clinical symptom formation, when discriminant statistical analysis was applied. The items on which the Indian patient group scored higher than the other two ethnic-cultural groups, were prolonged mourning reaction, suicide attempts, sociocultural identity confusion, marital maladjustment, alcohol or drug abuse, and violent acts against persons of the same group. In statistical comparison with patients from other backgrounds, symptoms of reactive depression were significantly more frequent in the Indian group, while indicants of schizophrenia and manic-depressive psychosis were exceedingly rare. Among male Indian patients, symptoms resulting from alcohol and/or drug abuse listed highest (70%), often with concomitant dysphoric moods. A remarkable number of female Indian patients showed symptoms of depression (76%); most had just gone through severely traumatizing experiences—a child had died in a fire, or a loved one had been murdered, had perished in an alcohol-connected accident, had drowned while fishing, etc.

It was in daily clinical experience with native patients, in discussion with native friends, and in consultation with native elders that the concept of *anomic depression* was formulated. The term *depression* was chosen to denote the prevailing symptom formation that is similar to reactive-neurotic depression in non-Indians, a "psycho-reactive disturbance" in Bleuler's (1975) sense, to be distinguished from "endogenous" conditions such as manic-depressive or schizophrenic psychosis, and from affective and cognitive disorder due to organic brain disease. However, while the clinical manifestations of anomic depression in the native patients were similar to those of reactive-neurotic depression in non-Indians, the underlying conflicts we uncovered in psychiatric interviews and with the help of testing devices were quite remote from the psychosexual complexes and Id-strivings of psychoanalytic theories. In these native patients we observed a clinical picture similar to neurotic depression, but the pathogenesis of this depression could not be explained in terms of a Freudian or Adlerian neurosis—its symptoms were not evolving from any frustration or repression of sexual impulses, nor from frustrated competitive strivings. Rather, the histories of these patients (see Chapter Four) revealed a sequence of typical life experiences from which developed a chronic dysphoric state, characterized by intense feelings of existential frustration, defeat, and lowered self-esteem. In crisis situations and under alcoholic disinhibition this state lead to discharges of randomly aggressive behaviour and/or suicidal action. The term *anomic* was chosen to denote the specific socio-cultural dynamics involved in the development of this psycho-reactive syndrome in North American Indians, dynamics different from those usually observed in non-Indian patients. They reflect the pathogenic effects of *anomie, relative deprivation* and *cultural confusion* as subjectively experienced in the particular context of the Indian-White relationship. Historically and contemporarily, the Indian-White relationship is characterized by an increasing dependency of the displaced aboriginal owners of the land on alien intruders who now constitute the majority society. This increasing dependency has undermined the sense of self-worth, purpose and dignity which gives meaning to human existence; it creates *existential frustration*, the pathogenic state of mind so well described by Viktor Frankl (1967, 1969). Indeed to suffer from anomic depression is to suffer from a life perceived as devoid of meaning in a specific socio-cultural context.

In a brief submitted to the Department of Health and Welfare, Canada, a Salish Indian consultant on native alcoholism stated:

> I am talking about the deaths of my people. I am talking about not only the deaths by accident, suicide and violence but also the death of the soul wh᠁ch lies behind the environment of self-destruction and despair in which Indian people exist as much today as a decade ago. It is my contention that the programs being funded through National Native Alcohol Abuse Program are not now and will not be effective until we can restore the sense of pride and power to the people and can begin to rebuild the shattered sense of self-worth, the effect of which is passed on from generation to generation. (Campbell 1980).

Rebuilding the shattered sense of self-worth in young Indian people is a major objective of the revived Salish Indian guardian spirit ceremonial. Since its revival among the Coast Salish, many a young native person has, through initiation and participation in the ceremonial, overcome anxiety and dysphoria, triumphed over alcohol and drugs, and thus escaped the fate of adding to the above cited mortality statistics as another casualty of anomic depression.[5] The Canadian public is only dimly cognizant of the extent of these casualty figures, and is hardly aware of the struggle against anomic depression waged by those Canadian Indians who turn to their traditional resources in the revived ceremonialism and in the new native Alcoholics Anonymous movement (cf. Jilek-Aall 1978). The

126

Canadian public was alerted by the media, however, to the three accidental deaths which occurred in 1972, 1974 and 1977 in connection with Salish spirit dance initiations in British Columbia; three among the hundreds who went through this arduous but often successful therapeutic enterprise in fifteen years. It was through these unfortunate incidents, widely publicized under sensational headlines, that many Canadians for the first time became aware of an ancient Indian ritual surviving in their neighbourhoods. The first accident in December 1972 brought indignant calls for legal intervention against the ceremonial. In a press interview published under the title "A curative Indian ritual or just a sadistic orgy?", a certain forensic psychiatrist declared, without having any firsthand information on either the case or the ritual, that:

> The danger in such ceremonies is that aggression and malevolence can easily take hold of the participants. . . . It becomes demonic and satanic. The breakdown of morality doesn't take too much. (The *Province,* February 20, 1973).

In the judicial inquests which followed each of the three incidents, I, together with Dr. Louise Jilek-Aall and Dr. Norman Todd, tried to focus public attention on the positive aspects of Salish spirit dancing. Without glossing over the tragedy of these accidental deaths, we suggested weighing them against the therapeutic benefits accruing to most participants in the guardian spirit ceremonial. At the inquest of February 21, 1974, in Chilliwack Court House, I stated:

> This ceremonial, commonly known as Salish spirit dancing, revived after a period of colonial suppression, attempts to turn the young people away from egocentric and asocial pursuits, away from liquor and illicit drugs which are taboo for all active dancers. . . . Initiation into the ceremonial aims at a total personality change. It aims at the candidate's reorientation towards the ideal norms of traditional Salish culture which had moral standards

127

superior to those of Euro-American civilization, as we know from reports of early ethnographers. Like all other effective methods of personality reorientation, this initiation treatment includes hard training and deprivations, in addition to teaching and exhortation. The candidate's motivation is tested in these trials in which he develops a stronger and healthier personality. I submit here that our Western society would be better prepared to meet the challenge of alcohol and drug abuse if we had similar culturally sanctioned methods available. That effective treatment procedures are not without risks will not surprise the psychiatrist who resorts to electro-shock in order to help a depressed patient. . . . The conclusion we have drawn is that many Indian patients are likely to benefit more from involvement in these native therapeutic activities than from exclusive contact with Western resources. We feel the persistence or revival of indigenous healing practices should be looked upon as an asset in the total health care for the Indian people to whom Western medical expertise is fully available in this area.

In all cases there was ample evidence that the deaths would not have occurred had there not been alcohol-induced damage to vital systems prior to resorting to Indian treatment. While none of the inquests could provide a basis for charges to be laid, much undeserved negative publicity for Salish spirit dancers and elders was created. They were left with the agonizing question of what are the alternatives which a majority society—itself unable to prevent, through its educational, legal, religious and medical institutions, the abuse of toxic agents by its own members—offers to young Indians at risk of alcoholic deterioration, drug addiction, suicide, or violent death?

128

1. Figures based on Canada Census and Indian Affairs data.

2. Data in this section is based on the Medical Services Annual Reports—Pacific Region, 1977, 1978, 1979 (Medical Services, Health and Welfare Canada, mimeographed brochures).

3. Note that in traditional Northwest Coast Indian cultures, fall and winter was the time of spiritual and social ceremonial activity, later largely eliminated by westernization.

4. *Panel presentation by native Community Health Representatives at the 4th Transcultural Workshop on Native Mental Health, Canadian Psychiatric Association, Vancouver, September 22-23, 1979.*

5. Follow-up information was obtained on twenty-one of the twenty-four "modern" spirit dancers on whom clinical data was presented in Chapter Seven. Eight years after the initial report (1972), 15 of these 21 spirit dancers (71%) had not relapsed into symptom formation or behaviour problems, and could be considered fully rehabilitated.

Chapter Eleven
Structure and Symbolism of Shamanic Healing

It was the demonstrated effectiveness of native treatment, comparing favourably with the available Western methods of medical-psychiatric and social-correctional management in cases of anomic depression among Indians, which prompted me, together with Dr. Louise Jilek-Aall and Dr. Norman Todd, to seek close cross-cultural collaboration with the traditional ritualists and healers of the Coast Salish area (cf. Jilek and Todd 1974; Jilek and Jilek-Aall 1978). We referred to our shaman colleagues those native patients in whom we recognized anomic depression as the underlying problem and who were amenable to indigenous approaches. Native patients, if so inclined, were seen by "Indian doctors" and ritualists while still in hospital. They attended healing rites on short leaves or underwent spirit dance initiation immediately after discharge, if that particular course was advised by the ritualists and supported by the sponsoring kinspeople. We came to respect the Indian elders' and healers' wisdom and skill in mobilizing the therapeutic resources of traditional native culture.

Close cross-cultural collaboration with indigenous healing resources is today advocated by many, practised by few, and still opposed by some. We were accused of "abandoning" the anomic depressive patient to the "mercies of the political and ceremonial leaders in Indian society" by Hippler (1980) who believes that psychosocial problems among native peoples are attributable to indigenous socialization which, in his opinion, "always gave, and still gives rise to the modally regressed personalities with which many of those Indian societies abound." To understand why such negative views on indigenous Indian society and ceremonialism can still be held today by the

130

editor of a scientific journal[1] we must consider an old and deeply engrained Western notion—that of the shamanic ritualist as a deviant, acting out his psychopathology in a sanctioned and prestigeful role. Prior to World War II, this was the prevailing view expressed in scientific treatises on the subject of American Indian healing ceremonials. Hambly (1926) suggested that shamanic healers are afflicted with psychiatric illness and characterized the Blackfoot Indian medicine man's garb as "mummery relieving the neurotic temperament of the performer." Wissler (1931), in his authoritative work on the American Indian, seriously proposed that the Indian shaman "may be a veritable idiot." The psychopathology hypothesis of shamanic healing derived mainly from confusing with mental illness the phenomenon which Eliade (1964) has termed *initiatory sickness* in the ecstatic initiation of shamanic ritualists, a stereotyped altered state of consciousness and behaviour that appeared rather bizarre in the prejudiced perception of Western observers. The seasonal *spirit illness* of future spirit dancers in aboriginal Coast Salish culture was such a pathomorphic (i.e. illness-like, but not pathologic) prelude to the exhibition of one's spirit powers in the dance ceremonial (see Chapter Three). The confusion of such culturally-conditioned ritualized behaviour with psychopathology gave rise to the "crazy witchdoctor" hypothesis, a eurocentric and positivistic fallacy, the history of which I have traced elsewhere (Jilek 1971).

Unfortunately this ideological leftover from nineteenth century colonialism has belatedly been elevated to undeserved scientific respectability by some prominent psychoanalytically-oriented anthropologists. No less a celebrity of American anthropology than Kroeber (1952) concluded from observations made mainly in aboriginal American Indian cultures that "not only the shamans are involved in psychopathology, but often also the whole lay public of primitive societies." Devereux, a distinguished author in the field of ethnopsychiatry, has been a most loyal adherent to the lunacy hypothesis of American Indian shamanism since he wondered in 1942, "how many

131

Indian psychotics have turned into shamans" while in mental hospitals? (Devereux 1942) In his most recent work (Devereux 1980) nothing is taken back from this summary diagnosing which he indulged in several decades ago. He again announces: "Briefly stated, my position is that the shaman is mentally deranged," and warns: "there is no reason and no excuse for not considering the shaman to be a severe neurotic or even a psychotic." (Devereux 1980, p. 14/15)

After years of personal and professional contact with traditional healers and shamans in North America and other parts of the world (Africa, Haiti, South America, Thailand and New Guinea), I consider this global pathology-labelling of the shaman to be absolutely untenable. It is still practiced by some psychoanalytically-oriented anthropologists, but is refuted by an increasing number of researchers in the field of cross-cultural psychiatry.

Through our collaboration with Salish ritualists we became aware of the semantic implications of indigenous nosology. Eventually we began to comprehend the symbol-language of Salish Indian ceremonials. The following presents an analysis of the structure and symbolism of these ceremonials in which, through skillful manipulation of culture-specific and collective symbols, psychotherapeutic effects are achieved.[2]

Strucure and Symbolism of Spirit Dance Initiation

Although in contemporary Coast Salish society, *spirit illness* is often fused with reactive depressive and psychophysiologic symptom formation in the context of anomic depression, its traditional semantic connotation has been preserved. The afflicted is said to be suffering from *syiwils təq'ǽ'q'ey*, "the spirit song's sickness". He is conceived of as being possessed by a wild, untamed power which could destroy him unless it is tamed and utilized as guardian spirit power. This power will benefit the patient only through initiation into spirit dancing; it is ambivalently perceived as beneficial to those who follow the traditionally prescribed "Indian ways" of dealing with it, but destructive to the resisting deviant. It is called *syiwil* in Eastern

132

Halkomelem, or *syə́wən* in Western Halkomelem dialects. These words are usually translated as "spirit song." They are derived from the root *yəw* meaning "having contact with the supernatural", and related to *yəwilmət* which is designatory of the shamanic ritualist who officiates at the initiation ceremonial. Together with his assistants, he helps the initiate-patient to "get out his spirit song" in order to manifest *syə́wən* power in the choreographic psychodrama of the spirit dance. The spirit song signifies and embodies the powers conferred on the spirit dancer in a guardian spirit vision experience called *su'lia* (Duff 1952) meaning "vision dream", or *s'ə́lyə* (Kew 1970) meaning "what you see in your dream". This is an altered state of consciousness induced in the initiate-patient by psychological, physiological, and physical means. In contemporary usage *syə́wən* denotes the essence of the whole guardian spirit ceremonial performed annually during the winter season. The sufferer from spirit illness is *q'a'q'əy,* dying sick.

His utter destruction is inescapable unless he submits to a vicarious ritualized "death" in the ordeal of spirit dance initiation, in which he is "grabbed" and symbolically "clubbed to death", only to be resurrected ("stood up again") and born again to a new life as a "baby", after a quasi-fetal period of regression while secluded under the nursing care of "baby-sitters".

According to one key informant, himself a leading ritualist and active spirit dancer for over fifty years, initiation implies rebirth and a "return from the dead"; drums and rattles are used extensively to "bring in the life spirit to the baby". The act of rebirth takes place when, after a gestation period of four days, the "song is found" and cried out by the baby, accompanied by the drumming and singing of the attendants. Then the baby is "run" through the woods, has a bath in the smokehouse, and submerges four times in an ice cold mountain stream which "brings the baby fully back to life". In contemporary spirit dance initiation, power is instilled by the ritualist and his "workers" who charge up to the initiate and "put their power"into him. As in Salish Indian doctoring, power is blown unto the initiate-patient by the shamanic healer whose *stɛqəm*, "breath, pregnant with power and vitality" (Robinson 1963 :105) appears synonymous with the archtypal breath of life (cf. Genesis 2:7).

While traditionally spirit power was acquired in an individual quest and later manifested and tamed in the initiation, it is now acquired by, and in, the initiation process, which at the same time constitutes the only treatment of spirit illness. One could therefore say that the newly found spirit song of the initiate can have two different meanings today; it is both an inheritance of the power quest, and a birth cry. There are two different systems, one the spirit power quest, the other the initiation which consists in being killed and reborn. The song occurs at the point where the two systems merge.[3]

The ambivalent character of the initiate spirit dancer—vulnerable and helpless yet also dangerous and powerful—is expressed symbolically in behaviour and paraphernalia. The initiate "babies" are considered dangerous, because they "have not yet learnt to control their power". They could easily "harm others without realizing it, by looking across at someone, wishing to have something of theirs or wishing for something to happen to that person." The babies' unregulated power is also revealed in dancing behaviour—they make wild jumps and disordered steps which have to be controlled by the efforts of the group of drummers and singers who accompany them. The initiates are at all times accompanied by "babysitters", also called "watchmen", whose duty is to both protect and check their charges. They hold on to a rope tied around the baby's waist. The initiates are "blind"—their eyes are covered by the long headdresses or by blindfolds—yet they are also "seeing". When guided by their power it is assumed that they can find their way around the smokehouse during the dance, bypassing people and bonfires. Their glance and their touch carry power; they must therefore avoid eye and body contact. Initiates are forbidden to "shoot" their power at others by pointing the finger at them. Unborn children are especially in danger from this strong and uncontrolled power and pregnant women are therefore urged to avoid any encounter with the initiates. One of the first White reporters on Coast Salish rituals, the Rev. Myron Eells in the 1870's, already observed the power-taming aspect of spirit dance initiation:

> Their dance consisted chiefly in running around with ropes encircling them, held by others. . . . I infer it was an initiatory custom with the black tamanous.[4] Some of them, I heard, were starved a part or all of the time. . . . Their faces were blacked in various ways. With the music of the drum and singing they jumped around in a space 20 feet in diameter, throwing their arms wildly about. . . . At the end of the house I saw four of the heads adorned with head-dresses of cloth strips. . . . Their bodies lay prone underneath the bed platform. Each one held down by a single man. . . . They evidently struggled to rise, and during the evening one did get up, and it required two or three men to put him down again (Eells 1889:664-7).

On the other hand, the initiate is vulnerable and has to be protected from other sources of power. His own spirit power is not yet solidly anchored in his body and can be "drawn out" easily by anything that is powerful. For this reason, he must avoid looking at powerful things which could "suck the spirit right out of the newborn baby". These taboos preclude looking at the sun, the fire, ritual objects such as the *sxwaixwe* mask, and dead bodies. Also forbidden is looking downstream, which is "towards death" (the land of the dead in Salish culture is traditionally situated in the direction of sunset, and it will be noted that in the Coast Salish area the course of major streams is from East to West). Initiates have to avoid any contact with menstruating women as "blood is too powerful". Spontaneous bleeding in general indicates the presence of a supernatural power, as exemplified in myths of the Salishan-speaking Bella Coola (Boas 1898). Initiates use straws when drinking from vessels which may have been handled by others, lest they risk the danger of spirit contamination. In logical consequence of

135

the taboo of contact with anything power-charged, they have to be wary of touching themselves, thereby causing a "short circuit" of power. For this reason they have scratcher-sticks to scratch their heads. Initiates must enter a place by moving backwards through the door in order to escape a surprise exposure to powerful things or persons. Strands of wool are placed around their wrists, ankles and waist in an effort to prevent the spirit power from being "drawn out of the newborn babies". The same method is resorted to in the case of a deceased person to prevent the premature release from the dead body of the spirit which might become dangerous to surviving kin at the home.

The spirit ceremonial neophytes are subjected to various diet taboos which, like many traditional prescriptions and proscriptions today, are rationalized by the younger generation in terms of physical hygiene. One important injunction exists against partaking of very hot or very cold food or beverage. Hot, steaming food was traditionally considered objectionable to spirits in Northwest coast cultures (cf. Drucker 1951:184). Very cold food is still felt to "take the life out of chest and stomach" where spirit power is thought to reside. Likewise, the initiate is cautioned against eating anything raw; he is given smoked, cooked or preferably dried foods, reminiscent of food in the land of the dead, which in Salish mythology consists of dried wood (cf. Adamson 1934:22). At the same time, this particular dietary prescription can be viewed as a symbolic move from nature to culture.

Once he has "found his song" (i.e., expressed his power publicly) the initiate is invested with his regalia, the new dancer's "hat" and "pole". This is expected to occur on the fourth day of initiation. The "hat" or headdress, made of thick, long woolen strands, is called *sayiws*, which derives from *sæy*, or "wool" and *-yiw* , meaning "having contact with the supernatural".[5] Before being placed on the "baby's" head, this headdress is subjected to a purification and power-charging ritual. It is purifed by being passed through fire four times, and charged with power from four fully-dressed spirit dancers who dance around the smokehouse with it and present it four times to each of the four corners. The recurrence of the magic number four of Salish mythology in this ritual undoubtedly ensures special potency. After four years of faithful adherence to the spirit dance ceremonial, the human-hair-headdress, *mǽqəl tə sayiws* (from *mǽqəl,* "human hair"), is bestowed on the mature spirit dancer as insignia of his responsibility. We may interpret this ascent from animal to human hair as graduation from an animal-like level of untamed, wild power to a human-like level of controlled and socialized power.

The new dancer's staff is *qáwə.* or the "cane of an infirm person", but it is also "like a canoe pole", and the neophytes are instructed to use the staff when walking as if "poling upstream", meaning "towards life". The long pointed staff is adorned at the top with paddles "for water", eagle feathers "for sky", deer hoofs "for animals", and cedar bark "for trees", so that "no part of the world is left out". Today, souvenir scarves are also attached and sometimes presented to the "witnesses" at the ceremonial as a special favour. The staff is made of a young spruce tree obtained by the ritualist from a high place in the mountains directly in the light of the rising sun, as he faces to the east from where life arises. The tree is carefully dug out with its roots intact, its bark is stripped, and its four top branches are cut short. In the smokehouse the chief ritualist or Indian Doctor "works" on the pole, burning the bottom in a fire "to make sure that it is really dead" and to purify it. He then paints four red rings ("red is life") on the top part and instills spirit power by blowing his breath onto it. In this way, the stick has been made to come alive again by the ritualist and is now "shaking by itself", which demonstrates that it is charged with spirit power. The neophyte taps this power by holding the shaking pole tightly with his two hands; he can "hear his song coming out of it". While dancing his tour, the new dancer leaves his staff with the baby sitters. Upon returning to his seat he immediately clings to it for strength and protection. At the end of the initiatory season, the new dancer's "pole" is deposited in a big hollow cedar far away from human habitation. In traditional times, this was the usual procedure with all ceremonial objects (Waterman 1930:547). Should his "pole" be found by someone, the new dancer would be in danger; should it be buried, he would die, as allegedly happened in a recent case. It is not difficult to recognize in the new spirit dancer's "pole" the archetypal maternal symbols of the Tree of Life and the World Tree, which is also the Tree of Rebirth (Jung 1952:368-419). As does its owner, the initiate's staff has to undergo the ritual ordeal of dying and being born again as a receptacle of power.

After four years of active participation in the ceremonial, the "grown up" spirit dancer qualifies to carry the k^w∂cmin$^{?}$, or "rattle stick", a club-like carved staff decorated with individual designs and deer-hoof pendants, the top end being a human or animal head. The mature dancer is well in control of his spirit power and no longer in need of ongoing protection. However, immediately after each dance tour even the senior ritualist feels vulnerable and holds on to his rattle stick for support. When this moment comes, the spirit dancer "cries like a baby because he is being born again, he is like a newborn baby again." Thus in every winter season and at every dance the spirit dancer relives, in attenuated form, the process of his past initiation, with spirit illness, death and rebirth. His individual dance and song manifest and express the spirit power he acquired and has learned to control.

Structure and Symbolism of the Power Board Ceremonial

A number of ethnographic reports on the Coast Salish mention shamanic spirits associated with a specific rite under the headings of $sg^u d\bar{i}'l\bar{a}tc$, $skudilitc$, $sk^w∂di'l∂c$, $sk^w∂ni'l∂\check{x}$, or $s.g^w∂dili\check{c}$ (Haeberlin and Gunther 1924; Wike 1942; Jenness 1955; Kew 1970; Amoss 1972; Collins 1974). The authors describe particular paraphernalia which may be used in this context: painted cedar boards, cedar poles, twisted cedar branches or cedar bark, and twisted vine maple. They are credited with the power of discovering lost persons and objects,

138

"smelling out" hidden things, clairvoyance, and recognition and cure of illness.

We observed the $sk^w \partial n\acute{\imath}l\partial\check{c}$ procedure on several occasions in the smokehouses of the Coast Salish, performed by Indian Doctors for diagnostic and therapeutic purposes during the winter ceremonial. The paraphernalia used in this ceremony consisted of either a pair of cedar boards or a pair of loop-shaped cedar branches or bark, bandaged with scarlet cloth similar to the "twisted ring of cedar bark in horseshoe shape" mentioned by Wike (1941:39). The "power boards" are rectangular cedar boards, approximately 30x45 cm, with slots by which they are held. They are painted black and white, showing the bare outline of either a mask-like face or a skeletonized figure. The following characteristics are attributed to the $sk^w \partial n\acute{\imath}l\partial\check{c}$ paraphernalia: they (1) have innate power; (2) move by themselves; (3) seek out their objects; and (4) have the capacity to cure.

An Indian Doctor of the highest reputation in the Coast Salish area, whose cooperation in the treatment of Indian patients we learned to appreciate, told us that he went on the quest for healing power at age thirteen. One day the sound of drumming guided him to a "trembling" cedar tree from which he obtained a $sk^w \partial n\acute{\imath}l\partial\check{c}$ song and eventually also his healing power. Later in life he returned to this tree to make a set of paraphernalia. He took some bark, shredded it, mixed it with red facial paint, and wrapped it with red cloth. By their own power the two sticks he had thus made twisted into a loop-shaped form. They have the power to "twist things and men", (i.e., to impose their innate twisting power on them). This Indian Doctor also commands the $sk^w \partial n\acute{\imath}l\partial\check{c}$ power of the cedar boards, the cedar branches, and the vine maple.

"Power poles" have been important instruments in $sk^w \partial n\acute{\imath}l\partial\check{c}$ ceremonies in the past, and a trio is said to be still in use on Vancouver Island. Our informants describe them as of different lengths up to ten feet, with some red cedar bark tied near the top end. The poles were held horizontally by the shaman's

139

assistants, who often had difficulty controlling the violent shaking movements, while the owner sang his song, accompanied by drumming. In behaviour, function, and ceremonial significance, the "power poles" are identical with the "power boards".

As author-observer descriptions of *sk^{W}aníláč* ceremonies are rarely encountered in ethnographic literature, I am presenting here a summary of our observations of contemporary *sk^{W}aníláč* rites.

The ceremonies were supervised by the Indian Doctor who owned the paraphernalia used on these occasions, either a pair of painted "power boards" or twisted "power sticks" (see sketches).The Indian Doctor in charge was assisted by other ritualists, by two groups of four ceremonial "workers", and by drummers and singers. Each instrument was carried by a pair of husky "workers" holding on to it with one hand and to a companion's belt with the other. The paraphernalia were "warmed up" at the bonfires in the smokehouse and "fed" by women, who threw pieces of smoked salmon and poured a little water into the flames. One after the other, the paraphernalia were carried around the smokehouse hall, facing the audience while people stood up in reverence. The instruments would then "smell the ground" and seemed to be magnetically attracted to each other, defying the "workers'" efforts to keep them apart. Rushing together and sweeping up high, the powerful tools would drag their guardians with them in a wild chase around the hall until their master, the Indian Doctor, intervened. Only he had the power to slow down and separate the unruly instruments. This procedure was repeated several times. The *sk^{W}aníláč* ran wild and the strong workers, in spite of desperate attempts to tame the instruments, were pulled around the hall, into each corner, out of the door and in again, lifted up and lowered to the ground in undulant movements. Again and again the power-charged instruments would pull together and had to be separated and pacified by the Indian Doctor who occasionally "blew power" into his hands before

140

touching them. From time to time, he held them close to his ears, listened attentively, and nodded his head. The instruments would then move around slowly, "smelling" and "searching", while the people watched in suspense. The $sk^w\partial n\hat{\imath}l\partial\check{c}$, just like the spirit dancer, is "blind" and yet seeing. The eyes painted on the power boards appear blind and the twisted power sticks are "blindfolded" by red cloth wrapped around them, and yet these paraphernalia point at and single out persons in the audience for recognition, reprimand, or treatment. In the $sk^w\partial n\hat{\imath}l\partial\check{c}$ curing rite, a sick person singled out by the paraphernalia would be quickly surrounded by relatives and friends. The power-laden tools would move up and down on all sides of the trembling patient, stroking him in gentle passes, and emanating their healing power while the Indian Doctor chants his song. At the end, with all drums beating, the $sk^w\partial n\hat{\imath}l\partial\check{c}$, in a final display of power, would chase its keepers four times around the smokehouse hall with such speed that the excited audience perceived them all as flying. The contemporary use of the $sk^w\partial n\hat{\imath}l\partial\check{c}$ paraphernalia as instruments of diagnosis and treatment in the broadest sense, as means to elicit and correct "wrong" conditions, will not readily provide cues about their origin, nor will enquiries with the ritualists. In ordinary "Indian Doctoring", the $sk^w\partial n\hat{\imath}l\partial\check{c}$ is not employed. We have to turn to older ethnographic sources on Coast Salish culture and to the etymology of Salish terms in order to reconstruct the derivation of this ceremonial and comprehend its symbolic significance.

All over the Northwest Coast area the ritual journey to the land of the dead in order to recover a lost or abducted soul or guardian spirit was performed by individual shamans with the help of their special spirit powers. In the form of a pantomime rite uniting the powers of a group of shamans in the effort to retrieve a patient's soul or guardian spirit, this shamanic voyage has been noted by culture element researchers among Coast Salish and Interior Salish populations (Barnett 1939; Ray 1942). It has also been noted among the Kwakiutl, Nootka, Tsimshian, and Haida (Drucker 1950).

Most of the ethnographic information on such collective shamanic expeditions to the realm of the ghosts was gathered in the southern Coast Salish area. As early as 1889, Rev. Eells (1889:677) reported on a big *tamanous* "power ceremony" of this kind in which eight Twana shamans, dismissed by the Reverend as "arrant humbugs", engaged in a pantomime trip to the land of the dead. Günther (1927:298) heard of a defunct ritual performance among the Klallam, called *sme'tnaq*, in which several shamans went to the land of the dead to recover a soul. This shamanistic performance was the famous Coast Salish spirit canoe ceremony, a curing rite of great antiquity, never witnessed by any of the area's ethnographers who described it under various related names: *smitinak*, Klallam (Curtis 1913); *sbEtEtda'q*, Snohomish (Haeberlin 1918); *sptda'q^W*, Dwamish (Waterman 1930); *smatnatc*, Lummi (Stern 1934); *spadak*, Puyallup-Nisqually (Smith 1940) *bɔsbɔ́tɔd'aq*, Twana, "soul-loss curers in a group soul recovery" (Elmendorf 1960); and *bɔ́ltadak*, Skagit (Collins 1974). The northern Puget Sound Salish word *sbɔtɔtdáq* is a duplication, indicating the continuous action or plural of the southern Puget Sound Salish term *spɔdák* and its equivalents, which are related to the Halkomelem word *spalɔq^W*, meaning "ghost".

Old Pierre, the Coast Salish shaman of the Lower Fraser Valley, told Jenness (1955:61-63) that the *sk^Wɔnílɔč* ceremony originated among the southern Coast Salish in the State of Washington. He said the *Sea sk^Wɔnílɔč* spirits travelled in canoes like the related *q^Wax^Wɔqs*. While the latter held up long poles, the former held boards in the air. In dancing, therefore, the protégés of either spirit carried power-charged poles or boards respectively, but both were serving the same purposes. If we follow Old Pierre's trace of the *sk^Wɔnílɔč* origin to the Puget Sound tribes in northern Washington, we read in Haeberlin and Günther (1924:59-64) about the *sg^udi'letc* board and the *q!woxq!* pole and their ritualized displays of power. The spirit in whose dance the cedar board was used was said to travel in a canoe. To the Puyallup-Nisqually (Smith

1940:114), *skwadilitc* suggested an object of inherent power which "could be used to go to the land of the dead to watch for souls".

In Dorsey's (1902) original account of the spirit boat and its function among the Dwamish, and in Waterman's (1930) detailed report, we note pictures of boards with handholds painted on the cedar planks of the spirit canoe. These are quite similar in shape to the power boards used today.[6] "Power entered these things during certain ceremonies and they dragged people about causing them to quiver and shake. The particular term for this object is *skudi'litc*," wrote Waterman (1930:302). There is also the closely related $q\mathcal{E}oxq\mathcal{E}$ spirit power which likewise jumps, quivers and drags the carrier of its pole around, and we recognize it as identical to the $q^waxq^w\partial qs$ pole-holding spirit of Old Pierre.

According to the original informants, the painted designs on the spirit-boat planks represent the shamans' spirit helpers travelling to the other world. They are surrounded by dots which stand for the "songs" revealed to the shaman by his particular spirit helper. On one of the planks (Dorsey op. cit. plate 64; Waterman op. cit. fig. 52, 53), the painting represents a spirit power "which can twist a victim into a knot". This twisting power is called *sxuda'tc* in Dwamish dialect. In his classical report on the Salish spirit canoe, Haeberlin (1918) related that there was a painted cedar board beside each man in the ceremony, owned by the shaman and depicting his vision experiences. The Snohomish term for these "magical boards" is rendered as *swan'c*. It will be noted that by inserting into the Dwamish *sxuda'tc* and the Snohomish *swan'c* the mystical suffix *íl*, which is used in Coast Salish languages to denote special supernatural relationships, terms equivalent to the Halkomelem *skᵂ∂níl∂č* can be derived. Shamanic power boards of Quinault medicine men were already described by Willoughby (1889:278); they were called "my doctor" or *se-guan* which is probably a lay transliteration of *sy∂w∂n*, spirit song and power. Curtis (1913) mentioned carved planks, representing vision experiences, which stood beside the bed of Coast Salish shamans.

Images with skeletal details found on shamanic boards and spirit canoe figures had already been recorded in drawings of Coast Salish planks by members of Wilke's United States Exploring Expedition 1838-1842 (Wingert 1949; plates 6, 7, 14, 21). To the old Quinault shamans, deer-hoof pendants attached to ceremonial objects signified "rattling bones" (Willoughby 1889:278). In the tradition of the Upper Skagit, the shaman used a "skeleton spirit" to diagnose soul loss and to assist him on the journey to the land of the dead to return the lost soul to its rightful owner (Collins 1974:201). In Amerindian cultures, we often find the shaman depicted in a "kind of x-ray style that goes back to Upper Palaeolithic times" (Furst 1973:33). Eliade (1964:63; 159) states:

> In the spiritual horizon of hunters and herdsmen bone represents the very source of life, both human and animal. To reduce oneself to the skeleton condition is equivalent to re-entering the womb of this primordial life, that is, to a complete renewal, a mystical rebirth. . . . The skeleton present in the shaman's costume summarizes and reactualizes the drama of his initiation, that is, the drama of death and resurrection.

I conclude, therefore, that the skeletonized design observed on modern Salish power boards is of very ancient origin and symbolizes the process of death and rebirth in the context of shamanic healing.

In the now obsolete Salish spirit canoe rite, each of the participating shamans carried a long staff or "magical pole" which was handled in the manner of canoe poles or paddles to propel the magic vessel to the land of the dead (Dorsey 1902:234; Waterman 1930:540; Haeberlin 1918:253). According to Dorsey and Haeberlin, the term for this pole among the Puget Sound Salish was *toucht'd* or *tsk!o'sEd* respectively, meaning "canoe pole". The Halkomelem equivalent is $\Theta k'^w \acute{o} \dot{s} \partial l$, from $\Theta k'^w \partial t$, meaning "to pull", a verb colloquially

144

used to denote propelling a canoe. When Wike (1941) collected her data in the northern Puget Sound area, the concept of the spirit canoe was gone, but the shaman travelling to recapture an individual's abducted spirit power still relied on his *suq̓o.'səd* cane, a term clearly equivalent to the above expressions. Among the Lummi, the southern neighbours of the Fraser River Salish, each of the medicine men enacting the spirit canoe ceremony took his position in the symbolic boat armed with a pole "just as he would were he to go out into the water" (Stern 1934:80). These poles were referred to as *qakwa*, which term takes us back to the *qʷaxʷəqs* spirits described by Old Pierre, who travelled in canoes, held long poles, and were associated with the Sea *skʷəníləč̌*.

In conclusion: the contemporary Salish *skʷəníləč̌* rite is a vestige of the ancient psychodramatic enactment of a collective shamanic boat journey to the land of the dead. The Salish spirit canoe of old retraced the voyage of the deceased person's soul, as it were, for in the past the dead were commonly buried in the southern Coast Salish area in a canoe which journeyed to the other world with them.[7] The grave canoe was placed on a support frame which held a special power for the recovery of abducted souls. This power was known by the term *sbətəda'q* (Elmendorf 1960:452), which also labels the spirit canoe ceremony.

Structure and Symbolism of "Indian Doctoring"

The Salish shaman or "Indian Doctor" is one who travels in search of a patient's lost soul or guardian spirit and restores it to the rightful owner. Consequently, his name, *šxʷlǽ·m*, derives from *šxʷəli-ae·m*, meaning "searcher of souls" and *šxʷɔ́l·əm*, meaning, "on one's course of travel".

Two basic disease concepts appear to have been brought from Central and Northern Asia to North America with consecutive waves of palaeolithic immigrants:
(1) Soul or spirit-power loss.
(2) Intrusion of a pathogenic object or spirit power into the patient.

Attending to these conditions has exclusively been the shamanic healer's business in Asia as well as in America (cf. Eliade 1964, ch. vii, ix). Hultkrantz (1953:448, 370), in his extensive review of the soul and spirit concepts of aboriginal North America, differentiates between *soul loss* and *spirit power loss*. In soul loss conditions, the "soul has disappeared or strayed to a place whence it cannot by itself return—e.g., the realm of the dead"—while spirit or power loss implies the "loss of a guardian spirit that is so intimately connected with the individual that his life is imperilled". The latter concept is especially characteristic of Puget Sound Coast Salish and some Interior Salish groups, but it is also found in such diverse populations as the Iroquois, Pawnee, Caddo, Shoshoni and Paviotso tribes and among New Mexico pueblos in the context of *nagualism*.

Soul loss and evil-agent intrusion as pathological theories and indications for shamanic soul recapture and evil-agent extraction were very widespread among the native peoples of Canada (cf. Margetts 1975). Culture element research in Northwestern America has depicted the following distribution: the soul-loss theory is universal among the northern Northwest Coast tribes and among the Gulf of Georgia Salish; in the Plateau area soul-loss illness is recognized mainly by tribal groups which do not recognize spirit loss illness, and vice versa. Intrusive objects or spirits as causes of disease are accepted by all northern Northwest Coast tribes, by nearly all Gulf Salish, and by most Plateau groups (cf. Drucker 1950; Barnett 1939; Ray 1942). Early references to soul loss by abduction among Coast Salish groups are made by Eells (1889:677):

> Sometimes before a person dies, it may be months, it is supposed that a spirit comes from the spirit world and carries away the spirit of the person, after which the person wastes away or dies suddenly. If by any means it is discovered that this has been done. . . then they attempt to get the spirit back by a tamanous, and if it is done the person will live;

and Wickersham (1898:346):

146

You might be asleep and your father who is dead might come and get your soul and take it to where the dead stay, across the river. Next day you would feel bad (sick) and grow worse, and finally die. . . . The soul may be separated from the body. The tamanous man can steal a soul away from the body and kill the person.

More recent descriptions of disease by soul loss, the intrusion of pathogenic agents, and of the shamanic cures of such conditions among the Coast Salish of British Columbia, have been presented by Barnett (1955:210-211) and Duff (1952:112-113). It is evident from their reports that the objects which were magically "shot" into the patient by evil shamans in order to cause illness were in fact animated power agents, and that there is no essential difference between the pathological theories of object intrusion and spirit intrusion. Today, the role of the few remaining "Indian Doctors" is viewed as geared to healing activity, and "shooting of power" is only attributed to the malevolent caprice of immature spirit dancers. In contemporary Salish *Indian Doctoring* the concepts of soul and spirit power are closely associated. It is believed that the spirit power may leave a person due to a sudden fright, as the soul was traditionally believed to do. Wike (1941), in her unpublished manuscript on southern Salish spirit dancing, categorizes loss of soul and loss of spirit power as separate conditions which, however, have the same cause—capture by shaman or ghosts and which call for the same therapeutic procedure—shamanic travel beyond this world and recapture of soul or spirit power; without this the patient will ultimately die.

According to our informants, loss of spirit power is mostly the result of inappropriate behaviour on the part of the owner. In one case, however, a girl's spirit power was taken away by a shaman upon her father's request, whereupon she instantly "died". In order to revive her, the shaman had to "put the spirit back there". We observed *Indian Doctoring* of patients suffering from psychogenic symptoms which were diagnosed as due to spirit intrusion and soul loss (cf. Jilek and Jilek-Aall 1978).

Structure and Symbolism of the *sxwaixwe* Ceremonial

Carved masks, of which there is an abundance in neighbouring regions of the Northwest Coast, are conspicuously absent in the Salish area. It is the more interesting, therefore, that a few families in the Fraser Valley region and the Gulf of Georgia have hereditary rights to a type of most elaborately carved wooden mask. This type of mask is of relatively recent origin, dating back only five or six generations (Duff 1952). Its extraordinary features are very different from those of other traditional masks of the Pacific Northwest. Comparison of earlier descriptions and pictorial representations of the *sxwaixwe* mask (Boas 1897; Curtis 1913; Stern 1934; Codere 1948; Barnett 1955) with more recently carved specimens shows that over many decades its strange appearance has changed very little: protruding peg-like eyes in a flat face dominated by a nose shaped like a bird's beak, a large hanging tongue, and one or two figures standing out like horns from the squarely-cut front, commonly representing birds, sometimes with human faces. The mask is surrounded by a wooden disk adorned with swan feathers. The *sxwaixwe* is used in a special dance ceremony performed in connection with the rites of puberty, marriage, and name giving, at the opening of a new smokehouse, or at other very important social occasions. The *sxwaixwe* dancer wears a white garment richly adorned with feathers. In one hand he holds a rattle of sea shells and in the other a pole or a cedar branch. The *sxwaixwe* rites that we observed on several occasions during recent years were surrounded by an aura of mysticism and danger. In view of the limited access of outsiders to this unique ceremony, a brief description of the contemporary *sxwaixwe* dance is presented here.

The dancers—strong young men chosen by the owner of the mask—prepare for the dance in a hidden enclosure in one corner of the smokehouse. With groaning noises and the sound of their shell rattles they indicate their readiness. Meanwhile the audience becomes increasingly excited; new spirit dancers present are hidden behind the backs of their "babysitters" and

148

wrapped in blankets to be shielded from the powerful spirit of the *sxwaixwe*. A selected group of women gathers on the side opposite to the enclosure, ready to drum and sing. Finally, the masked dancers burst forth from their confinement and chase around with violent movements and rapid steps, howling, shaking their rattles and swaying their masks as they dance around the hall of the smokehouse, presenting a frightening spectacle. When the female chorus sets in with a melodious song and slow rhythmic drumming the ferocious *sxwaixwe* immediately calm down, stepping heavily in time with the slow rhythm, swinging their rattles in a slow but forceful movement. As soon as the women stop singing, the *sxwaixwe* run wild again, while the spectators react with fear and awe. Again the women repeat their soothing song that pacifies the wild dancers. During the calm periods, people hasten to put some coins in the dancers' hands, carefully avoiding touching the *sxwaixwe* costume. Finally, the women's forceful drumming and singing compels the dancers to disappear behind the walls of their confinement, but three times the unruly *sxwaixwe* sally out and chase around again until at the fourth attempt they are ultimately overpowered by the women's song. The watchers sigh with relief once the last *sxwaixwe* dancer has disappeared.

Each family with hereditary rights to a mask has a story explaining its origin and can name the exact place where the mask was procured. There are two opposing clusters of origin myths. On Vancouver Island, the *sxwaixwe* is supposed to have come down from the sky, while on the mainland of British Columbia it is said to have been fished out of the sea or out of a lake. Ethnographic sources suggest, however, that the first *sxwaixwe* mask originated from somewhere up the Fraser River (Barnett 1939; Duff 1952). The name of the mask appears in *sxʷā.yxʷeyla*, anglicized as *Squiala*, or "place of the *sxwaixwe*", which is the name of a Coast Salish Indian band and of a locality in the vicinity of Chilliwack, British Columbia.

In his comparative analysis of *sxwaixwe* masks and numerous versions of the *sxwaixwe* myth among neighbouring Coast

Salish tribes, Lévi-Strauss (1975; 1979) conclusively demonstrates that the *sxwaixwe* occupies a central place in Salish culture. Its bird-fish configuration corresponds to the two basic origin myths—the feather costume, the nose in the form of a bird's head or beak, and the two bird heads on top represent the sky realm; the fish-shaped tongue and shell rattles represent the aquatic realm. In some versions of the myth, the *sxwaixwe* is connected with a certain fish, or with women changing into a certain fish, which Lévi-Strauss (1975) has identified as a deep water rock fish, the Red Snapper, of the *Sebastodes ruberrimus* species.[8]

Lévi-Strauss has revealed the mask's pre-eminent role in society. Beyond its functions in the service of individual owners, the *sxwaixwe* mask is the mediator of exogamous marriage. His interpretation is corroborated in the story told by a key informant in which the appearance of the *sxwaixwe* among the Scowlitz Indians of the Upper Fraser Valley changed the abnormal social and sexual attitudes of two sisters and their brother. The *sxwaixwe* has shamanic healing power as well, and this will become readily apparent from a brief summary of mainland versions of the origin myth. These versions relate how a young man, afflicted with a smelly skin disease, feels rejected and ridiculed and decides to end his life. Arriving at a lake or stream, he jumps into the water with the intention of drowning himself. Instead, he recovers consciousness and finds himself on the roof of a house. He is invited in by the water spirit people and asked to cure the chief's daughter or some other sick person there. He recognizes that the illness is caused by the spittle or the tears which he had dropped into the water. He cures the sick person, and in some versions he marries the chief's daughter. In every version he is given the *sxwaixwe* mask, which has to be fished out of the water by his sister who must use her own hair as fishline. On returning home, the hero is cured of his skin disease. He has now become a shaman himself, endowed with the power to cure certain illnesses. His sister marries and is given the mask as a dowry;

the mask brings its owners good luck and riches. Some versions state that whenever the men dance with the *sxwaixwe* there is an earthquake, a reference to the chthonian powers of the mask (Lévi-Strauss 1975).

In contemporary Coast Salish culture the *sxwaixwe* rite is often performed in conjunction with the winter spirit dances. Barnett (1955) and Lévi-Strauss (1975; 1979) draw attention to the rule that the *sxwaixwe* dancers must not at the same time be spirit dancers and maintain that the *sxwaixwe* rite is not part of the winter ceremonial. Yet it is obvious from the myths of origin that the mask is thought of as having supernatural properties, and that it bestowed shamanic curing power on its first owner. The young man who received the mask is presented as being at the age of, or in the process of, training for his spirit quest (Boas 1894; Stern 1934; Codere 1948). He falls ill, and in order to be cured he has to go through the initiation experience of death and rebirth. He drowns (i.e., he journeys to a beyond which is under water), encounters water spirits, and is reborn, coming out of the water[9] and returning home with the *sxwaixwe* mask, the representation of the spirit power he has acquired.

In some versions the hero is depicted as bathing and purifying himself for many days before he jumps into the water (Jenness 1955:91) in the manner of those questing for spirit power. In others he goes swimming and diving every day in order to become strong (Boas 1894:455); he lies down by the water to sleep and has a dream-vision of two spirit helpers, who advise him what to do in order to be cured and who impose food taboos on him (Stern 1934; Jenness 1955). Some versions relate that the hero has been away for four days or for four years (Smith 1938; Codere 1948), which are the traditional time spans in the Salish spirit dance initiation process. Before he re-enters the parental home, his kinspeople must clean themselves and the house and place new mats where the returning hero will stay (Stern 1934). The same procedure was followed whenever a shaman came home with newly-acquired spirit power. Most versions relate that he was cured after having healed the underwater people and that he knew medicines and could cure certain diseases upon his return (Codere 1948). The hero thus has become an Indian Doctor—he can make people sick, but can also cure them (Hill-Tout 1902). The boy who is to receive the *sxwaixwe* has been singled out in his family, which is often the case with shamans-to-be. He is afflicted with a skin disease, a condition often attributed in North American Indian myths to a hero who, at first rejected, subsequently acquires supernatural powers stronger than anybody else's. In the version related to us by a prominent local owner of the mask, the hero's previously unsocialized attitude is epitomized in the traditional text of the *sxwaixwe* song which states that he had a "stomach of stone".[10] Through the *sxwaixwe* experience he undergoes a personality change, a social cure such as is also effected by the spirit dance initiation. In the spirit quest, the initiate sees his ceremonial attire and face painting in a dream or vision; in this version of the *sxwaixwe* myth an Indian Doctor is called in and has a vision of the *sxwaixwe* costume to be worn with the mask.

It appears that the shamanistic properties of the *sxwaixwe* mask have been lost and that it has been taken out of the spirit ceremonial complex where it undoubtedly once belonged. However, the power inherent in the mask is still believed to be so strong that the vulnerable new spirit dancers present at the *sxwaixwe* ceremonial must be shielded and protected from its influence. This power may be seen as deriving from the stark combination of binary oppositions symbolized in the mask itself, in the ceremonial costume, and in the choreographic drama of the *sxwaixwe* rite. The bird-fish nature of the mask, combining the aerial and aquatic realms, is repeated in the costume—the dancer is adorned with feathers while holding seashell rattles.

Most conspicuous in the *sxwaixwe* rite is the antagonism of the sexes. The wild power of the male dancers—only strong young men can perform the *sxwaixwe* dance—is tamed by the women's peaceful, soothing song which imposes order and

152

rhythm on chaotic energy. In agreement with Lévi-Strauss' interpretation of the *sxwaixwe* (1975), I summarize in conclusion: on the level of cosmos and nature, *sxwaixwe* is a mediator of distant elements, joining heaven and earth, sky and water, bird and fish. On the level of human society, *sxwaixwe* is a mediator between distant kin groups, joining man and woman in exogamous marriage (brother gives mask to sister when sister marries into another band), and also joining distant tribes in ceremonial functions at which the *sxwaixwe* mask is displayed. Lévi-Strauss has turned our attention to the fact that the peculiar form of the mask resembles the shape of the copper plates used so extensively at Northwest Coast potlatches. This further emphasizes the mediator role of the *sxwaixwe* in the exchange of wealth between social units. Its function is equivalent to that of the copper plates, which were symbols of riches and the main objects in the exchange of wealth among the coastal tribes north of the Salish area. Beyond the mask's important mediator functions, the myth attests to its shamanic origin and power, which is still manifested in the contemporary ritual.

Structure and Symbolism of Shamanic Ceremonials in Salish Culture

The same basic symbolism and the same structural pattern can be recognized in all four types of rituals.

Basic Symbolism: Shamanic Journey to the Land of the Dead.

Very aptly, the Halkomelem Salish term for shaman, $\check{s}x^w l\grave{a}\cdot m$, is derived from the verb *læm*, "to go"; he is "the one on his course of travel". In his therapeutic pursuits, the shaman travels to the other world, to the Land of the Dead from whence only return those who have acquired shamanic powers. Eliade (1964) has demonstrated the universality of the shamanic journey to the "underworld" for the recovery of a soul or guiding spirit in the cultures of North and South America, Central and North Asia.

153

This shamanic voyage is most conspicuous in the *skʷəni'ləč* rite, which derives from the now obsolete spirit canoe ceremony, and in *Indian Doctoring*, in which a lost soul or guardian spirit is fetched from the Land of the Dead "across the river". The *sxwaixwe* myth combines the shamanic travel to another world under water with the hero's cure and shamanic initiation. It thus repeats a general theme of North American Indian mythology (cf. Eliade 1964:312). Salish spirit dance initiation, with its leitmotif of death and rebirth, implies the novice's travel to the Land of the Dead. His journey starts when he is "clubbed to death", and he does not return fully to the land of the living until he has found his spirit song. He then re-emerges to live a healthier and socially more rewarding existence. Like the shamans in the spirit canoe, the initiate is highly vulnerable. While on his trip, he must be protected by "babysitters" and by his uniform and staff. With the staff he "poles upstream, toward life" in the same manner as the spirit canoe voyageurs.[11] The initiate has to fast and must resist the temptation of accepting food with which he is "teased", for the myths tell him that he who accepts food in the Land of the Dead will remain there forever. The mature spirit dancer relives this archetypal journey at every winter ceremonial. In a trance, he dances around the hall of the smokehouse which always extends in east-west direction, "looking to the Land of the Dead".[12] Although blindfolded, he finds his way past obstacles just as does the shaman on his voyage to the other world. The spirit dancer has to beware of stumbling or slipping, which augurs ill, as would a shaman's misstep or fall during the spirit canoe ceremony. When returning to his seat the dancer feels rejuvenated "like a newborn baby".

The Salish concept of power implies an inherent ambivalence due to the combination of binary-opposed destructive and constructive forces.[13] Resolution is achieved through shamanic ritual intervention, which tames the potentially dangerous power and transforms it into constructive, therapeutic power which can be used beneficially. Without such intervention, the destructive, pathogenic potential of supernatural power is realized to the detriment of the individual.

In reference to Lévi-Strauss' (1963) ideas on the effectiveness of symbols, we may assume that the confirmed therapeutic effects of Salish ceremonials are achieved through the use of collective symbols that are patterned in accordance with neuropsychologically-determined structural laws, and that therefore have direct access to the unconscious.

STRUCTURAL PATTERN:

A dialectic process of supernatural power in the four types of ritual activity.

	Power Acquisition	Power Manifestation	Power Taming	Power Utilization
Indian Doctoring	Shaman's quest for healing power	Shaman's initiatory sickness	Shamanic initiation ordeal; intervention by senior shamans	Treatment of soul and guardian spirit loss and of spirit intrusion
Power Board and Pole Ceremonial	Shaman's quest for *skʷəníʔləč* power; ritual preparation of paraphernalia	Display of "wild" power of paraphernalia	Manipulation of paraphernalia by shaman in *skʷəníʔləč* ceremony	Diagnosis: "smelling out" and "searching" power; Therapy: transfer of healing power from paraphernalia to patient
Spirit Dance Initiation	Spirit quest; Power appears in dream-vision; Finding of song	Spirit illness; Display of "wild" power of new spirit dancer	Spirit dance initiation ordeal; Intervention by ritualist, workers, babysitters, drummers	Therapeutic, social, economic benefits of guardian spirit power
sxwaixwe Ceremonial	Mythical quest hero's acquisition of mask; (later by inheritance)	Display of "wild" power of *sxwaixwe* dancers (male)	Intervention by chorus (female) in *sxwaixwe* ceremony	In myth: therapeutic, social and economic benefits; In ceremonial: social and economic benefits of *sxwaixwe* power

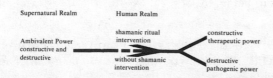

Supernatural Realm   Human Realm

Ambivalent Power constructive and destructive ➤   shamanic ritual intervention   constructive therapeutic power

without shamanic intervention   destructive pathogenic power

155

Footnotes:

1. *The Journal of Psychological Anthropology, New York.*

2. I am indebted to Dr. Louise Jilek-Aall, Dr. Norman Todd and Dr. Brent Galloway for their assistance in preparing this analysis. I am most grateful to Chief Richard Malloway of Sardis, B.C., and to Mr. Isadore Tom of Lummi, Washington, who provided the pertinent ethnographic and linguistic information.

3. *Discussion comments by Professor C. Lévi-Strauss, July 9, 1974.*

4. From *tomanoas,* the gloss given as a Cowichan term for "guardian spirit" by Captain Wilson (1866:281).

5. The Musqueam have another term for the initiate's hat, *sxa'yus* (Kew 1970:163), which is reminiscent of Puget Sound *skayu,* meaning "inhabitant of the land of the dead" (Haeberlin 1918:254), again evoking the death-rebirth theme.

6. cf. illustrations in Dorsey, op. cit. plates 65, 66; Waterman op. cit. fig. 54, 147; Wingert 1949, plate 16.

7. For comparative ethnological data on the association of the nearly universal idea of the "Boat of the Dead" with that of the "Shamanic Boat", see Eliade 1964:355-358.

8. Dr. Louise Jilek-Aall noticed while scuba fishing that the eyes of the Red Snapper bulge out when this fish is brought to the surface, a phenomenon caused by pressure differences. It may well be that the protruding eyes of the *sxwaixwe* mask symbolize the Red Snapper which is looked upon as a supernatural being by several Northwest Coast Indian tribes.

9. cf. Jung (1952) for the rebirth symbolism of emergence from water in Old World mythology and Judaeo-Christian religious traditions.

10.According to Chief Richard Malloway, the expression "stomach of stone" implies that the hero had a negative social disposition; he was not communicating with, and had little concern for, his people. In discussion, Professor Lévi-Strauss has commented that this expression is reminiscent of what is said about the Coeur d'Alêne Indians of Idaho, namely, that they have a heart as tiny as a bird's and very hard, because they are considered to have a mean disposition. Linguistic evidence from related Salish languages suggests that the suffix for "stomach" is used to signify emotional states, such as the Thompson Salish word *k'əs-aenk*, "angry", which literally means "bad stomach". Mythological evidence suggests that in this particular case the hero's father was the tribal ancestor who had been changed into stone by the Transformer *Xals*, which as a rule was inflicted upon a person as punishment for misdeeds. The father's meanness is also indicated by his name, which contains the prefix *qel-*, meaning "bad" (for details of the myth see Boas 1895:27).

11.According to Waterman (1930:556), the spirit canoe rite was linked with spirit dance initiation through a special spirit power, *Xe'dxedib*.

12.Shamans travelling in the spirit canoe were facing west when on their way to the Land of the Dead, and facing east when returning to the living world. The spirit canoe ceremony could therefore only be performed in a house lying in the direction of east and west (Haeberlin 1918:252).

13.cf. C.G. Jung (1952:654, 747) on the archetypal *coincidentia oppositorum*, the ambivalent union of opposites, which is seen as generating the dynamic tension of psychological extremes and which leads to release of energy.

Chapter Twelve
Renaissance of North American Indian Ceremonialism

Salish spirit dancing is but one example of the traditional ceremonials which have in recent decades been revived or adopted by North American Indian peoples. Other examples are the Sun Dance, the Gourd Dance, and Peyotism. These have many features in common with Salish spirit dancing and likewise hold considerable therapeutic potential. Since about 1960, the revived cult dance movements, as the peyote cult before, have become foci of native identity and carriers of a pan-Indian message, serving psychosocial healing functions for the individual and the collective under the direction of skillful ritualist leaders.

The Sun Dance ceremonial, which had survived on a small scale among the Ute and Shoshone, was revitalised in the late 1950's and became the major religious movement of Indian tribes in Wyoming, Idaho, Utah, and Colorado (Jorgensen 1972). The Sioux Sun Dance has also experienced a revival in the 1960's, with hundreds of participants gathering annually in August for the ceremonial at Pine Ridge reservation; the formerly outlawed self-torture is again practiced. As in the Salish Spirit ceremonial, Sun Dancers must abstain from alcohol and from drug intake for extended periods; they must adhere to traditional rules of conduct in order to acquire and control the supernatural "Indian power", a positive spiritual force which the emerging pan-Indian opposition mythology compares to the negative materialism of White society in a series of binary juxtapositions. As we had occasion to observe at Salish spirit dances, such nativistic culture propaganda has identity and ego-strengthening therapeutic effects on many culturally drifting young native persons who are at risk of *anomic depression* and alcohol abuse. Again in analogy with Salish spirit dance initiation, the emphasis in the Sun Dance is on the acquisition of supernatural power for one's own well-being and that of one's people, in a ritual which has the characteristic features of shamanic initiation— calling and instruction by dream visions, guidance and teaching by a shamanic ritualist, ordeals in quest of a personal power vision finally received in an altered state of consciousness. Fasting, thirsting, pain, and privation as well as high intensity rhythmic drumming, in frequencies which can be expected to evoke auditory driving responses in the human brain, are used in both ceremonials to facilitate entry into the altered state of consciousness so important for achieving lasting personality changes.

Similar intensive sensory stimulation by rattling and drumming is also a feature of the Gourd Dance, which was restarted among the Kiowa in the 1950's. Gourd Dance singers formed new inter-tribal societies among the Kiowa, Comanche, Cheyenne and Arapaho during the 1960's and carried the ceremonial from Western Oklahoma to many plains and prairie tribes in the United States and Canada. By 1975, it had spread south to the Navajo, north to the Blackfoot and Cree, and northeast to the Ojibwa and Dakota Sioux. The "classical Indian" style of the Gourd Dance and the articulation of nativistic sentiments in its songs—some have become hits— appeal to the younger native generation striving beyond a tribal and toward a pan-Indian cultural identity. Gourd Dance sessions, as those of the Salish spirit dances, provide partici-pants with meaningful collective activity, ego-strengthening group support, and an opportunity for socially sanctioned emotional abreaction. Excitement builds during "fast songs", when drumming and rattling tempo increases, leading to psychodramatic discharges of aggressive feelings accumulated under acculturative stress. These effects may play a role in the prevention and alleviation of *anomic depression*, for the Gourd Dance ceremonial is credited with rehabilitating many partici-

159

pants who had become despondent alcoholics (Howard 1976).

The Peyote Cult, first described by the learned Franciscan Bernardino de Sahagún in Mexico in 1560 (Sahagún, ed. 1977), spread northward to many North American Indian tribes in the wake of the nativistic Ghost Dance in the late 1800's. By the mid-1950's, it had become the major pan-Indian religious movement in the U.S. and Canada east of the Rocky Mountains, a therapeutic movement in which restoring and preserving the individual member's health opens the prospect for successful restoration and preservation of native culture. The therapeutic aspects of Peyotism are well documented and have been reviewed elsewhere (cf. Jilek 1978). One of the avowed purposes of the cult is to combat alcoholism among Indians. Its safety and efficacy in doing so has been attested to by scholars and experienced clinicians, among them Karl Menninger, who sees in peyote "a better antidote to alcohol than anything the missionaries, the White man, the American Medical Association, and the Public Health Service have come up with" (Bergman 1971). In an epidemiological survey among Indians in Saskatchewan, Roy et al. (1970) observed that rehabilitated former alcohol abusers on different reservations invariably attributed their non-drinking to participation in the Peyote Cult. However, the safe therapeutic factor in the Peyote Cult is not the hallucinogenic cactus *Lophophora williamsii Lemaire* which is used, but the psychotherapeutic nature of the cult. Comparable results are achieved in the spirit dance ceremonial of the Coast Salish who never adopted Peyotism and insist on acquiring wholesome "Indian power" without resorting to psychotropic agents.

Considering the unquestioned superiority of Western science, the negative attitude of educators, law makers and law enforcers, and the hostility previously shown by the churches, it is surprising that, after 100 to 300 years of Euro-American dominance, any of the indigenous ceremonials in North America should have survived the "zeal of the missionaries, the scorn of the unthinking, and the curiosity of anthropologists"

160

(Attneave 1974.) Even more surprising is the increasing interest and participation in such ceremonials by semi-urbanized and Western-educated North American Indians. The persistence and revival of indigenous healing ceremonials can certainly *not* be attributed to a lack of modern treatment services; it has more to do with a lack of culture-congenial and holistic approaches in modern medicine, such as those conceptualized by transcultural psychiatry and psychosomatic medicine but still not generally applied in practice. The native view of what makes the difference between modern Western medical practices and traditional North American Indian healing has been succinctly stated by the Mohawk Elder, Ernie Benedict (1977):

> The difference that exists is that the White doctor's medicines tend to be very mechanical. The person is repaired but he is not better than he was before. It is possible in the Indian way to be a better person after going through a sickness followed by the proper medicine.

While accepting the evident need for culture-congenial group psychotherapeutic approaches as a significant factor contributing to the revival of North American Indian ceremonialism, the historian may wish to look for underlying causes explaining the synchronicity of the revivals. They all occurred between the mid-1950's and the late 1960's, which was the era of global decolonization and geopolitical retreat by Western powers. These historical processes were reflected in profound changes in the prevailing *Zeitgeist*. The once glorious Western self-image was deflated, the once dominant eurocentric world view abandoned. Western superiority claims were relinquished in favour of an upgrading of the Western image of non-Western cultures, in particular the image of American Indian cultures. It was in such a changing climate that native people turned to their own heritage, and that health professionals came to recognize the value of native therapeutic resources.

161

References

Aberle, David F.
  1966   The Peyote Religion Among the Navaho. Chicago: Aldine.
Ackerknecht, Erwin H.
  1943   Psychopathology, Primitive Medicine and Primitive Culture. Bulletin of the Institute of the History of Medicine 14:30-67.
Adamson, Thelma, ed.
  1934   Folk-tales of the Coast Salish. Memoirs of the American Folklore Society. Vol. 27. New York: Stechert.
Adrian, E.D. and B.H.C. Matthews
  1934   The Berger Rhythm, Potential Changes from the Occipital Lobes in Man. Brain 57:355-385.
Altman, George J.
  1947   Guardian Spirit Dances of the Salish. Masterkey for Indian Lore and History 21:155-160.
Ames, Michael M.
  1957   Reaction to Stress, A Comparative Study of Nativism. Davidson Journal of Anthropology 3:17-30.
Amoss, Pamela T.
  1972   The Persistence of Aboriginal Beliefs and Practices Among the Nooksack Coast Salish. Doctoral Thesis, Dept. of Anthropology, University of Washington, Seattle.
Attneave, Carolyn L.
  1974   Medicine Men and Psychiatrists in the Indian Health Service. Psychiatric Annals 4:49-55.
Ayd, Frank J.
  1961   Recognizing the Depressed Patient. New York: Grune and Stratton.
Barber, T.X.
  1958   The Concept of 'Hypnosis'. Journal of Psychology 45:115-131.
Barnett, Homer G.
  1938   The Coast Salish of Canada. American Anthropologist 40:118-141.

1939   Culture element distributions IX: Gulf of Georgia Salish. Anthropological Records Vol. 1. No. 5. Berkeley: University of California Press.

1955   The Coast Salish of British Columbia. Eugene, Oregon: University of Oregon Press.

1957   Indian Shakers, A messianic Cult of the Pacific Northwest. Carbondale, Illinois: Southern Illinois University Press.

Benedict, E. and T. Porter
1977   Native Indian Medicine Ways. Monchanin Journal 10:17-22.

Benedict, Ruth F.
1923   The Concept of the Guardian Spirit in North America. Memoirs of the American Anthropological Association No. 29.

Bergman, Robert L.
1971   Navajo Peyote Use: Its apparent safety. American Journal of Psychiatry 128:695-699.

Bilz, Rudolph
1966   Der Vagus-Tod. Die Medizinische Welt 17:117-122; 163-170.

Bleuler, Manfred
1960   Lehrbuch der Psychiatrie. Berlin: Springer. (10th edition)

1961   Bewusstseinsstoerungen in der Psychiatrie. In Bewusstseinsstoerungen, H. Staub and H. Thölen, Eds. Stuttgart: Thieme.

1975   Lehrbuch der Psychiatrie. Berlin: Springer. (13th edition)

Boas, Franz
1894   The Indian Tribes of the Lower Fraser River. Report of the 64th Meeting of the British Association for the Advancement of Science, 1894:454-463.

1895   Indianische Sagen von der Nord-Pacifischen Küste Amerikas. Berlin: A. Ascher.

1897   The social organization and the secret societies of the Kwakiutl Indians. Report of the U.S. National Museum for the year ending June 30, 1895. *In* Annual Report of the Board of Regents of the Smithsonian Institution. Pp. 311-738. Washington: Government Printing Office.

1898   The Mythology of the Bella Coola Indians. Publications of the Jesup North Pacific Expedition 2. *In* Memoirs of the American Museum of Natural History. Vol. 2: Anthropology, i. New York: Knickerbocker Press.

Burns, B.H.
1971   Breathlessness in Depression. British Journal of Psychiatry 119:39-45.

Campbell, Wilbur T.
1980   Brief on National Native Alcohol Abuse Programs. Submitted to the Department of Health and Welfare, Canada; Mimeograph, 18pp.

Cannon, Walter B.
1942   "Voodoo" Death. American Anthropologist 44: 169-181.

Clemhout, Simone
1964   Typology of Nativistic Movements. Man 64:14-15.

Codere, Helen
1948   The *sxwaixwe* Myth of the Middle Fraser River. The Integration of Two Northwest Coast Cultural Ideas. Journal of American Folklore 61:1-18.

Collins, June McC.
1950   The Indian Shaker Church, A Study of Continuity and Change in Religion. Southwestern Journal of Anthropology 6:399-411.

1974   Valley of the Spirits: The Upper Skagit Indians of Western Washington. The American Ethnological Society Monograph 56. Seattle: University of Washington Press.

Collomb, Henri
  1965   Assistance psychiatrique en Afrique, experience sénégal-
          aise. Psychopathologie africaine 1:11-84.
Curtis, Edward S.
  1913   Salishan Tribes of the Coast, The Chimakum and the
          Quilliute, the Willapa. The North American Indian
          9. Norwood, Mass. (Edition cited: New York, Johnson
          Reprint Corporation, 1970.)
Davis, P.A., Davis, H., and J.W. Thompson
  1938   Progressive Changes in the Human Electroencephalo-
          gram under Low Oxygen Tension. American Journal
          of Physiology 123:51-52.
Devereux, George
  1942   The Mental Hygiene of the American Indian. Mental
          Hygiene 26:71-84.
  1980   Basic Problems of Ethnopsychiatry. Chicago: Univer-
          sity of Chicago Press.
Dorsey, George A.
  1902   The Dwamish Indian spirit boat and its use. Bulletin
          of the Free Museum of Science and Art of the
          University of Pennsylvania 3:227-238.
Driver, Harold E.
  1969   Indians of North America. Chicago: University of
          Chicago Press.
Drucker, Philip
  1950   Culture element distributions XXVI. Northwest Coast.
          Anthropological Records. Vol. 9. No. 3. Berkeley:
          University of California Press.
  1951   The Northern and Central Nootkan tribes. Smithsonian
          Institution Bureau of American Ethnology Bulletin
          144. Washington: Government Printing Office.
Du Bois, Cora
  1939   The 1870 Ghost Dance. Anthropological Records
          Vol. 3:1, Berkeley: University of California Press.

165

Duff, Wilson
  1952 The Upper Stalo Indians of the Fraser Valley, British
        Columbia. Anthropology in British Columbia Memoir
        1. Victoria: Provincial Museum of British Columbia.
Durkheim, Emile
  1897 Le suicide. Paris: Alcan.
  1915 The Elementary Forms of the Religious Life. London:
        Allen and Unwin.
Eells, Myron
    1889 The Twana, Chemakum, and Klallam Indians of
          Washington Territory. *In* Annual Report of the
          Board of Regents of the Smithsonian Institution for
          the year ending June 30, 1887. Part 2:605-681.
          Washington: Government printing Office.
Eliade, Mircea
  1964 Shamanism, Archaic Techniques of Ecstasy. London:
        Routledge and Kegan Paul.
Ellenberger, Henri F.
  1951 Der Tod aus psychischen Ursachen bei Naturvolkern
        ('Voodoo Death'). Psyche 5:333-344
Elmendorf, William W.
  1960 The Structure of Twana Culture. Washington State
        University Research Series Monograph Supplement
        2. Pullman: Washington State University Press.
Erikson, Erik H.
  1950 Childhood and Society. New York: Norton.
Ey, Henri
  1963 Manuel de Psychiatrie. Paris: Masson.
Frank, Jerome D., and Florence Powdermaker
  1959 Group Psychotherapy. *In* American Handbook of
        Psychiatry 2, Silvano Arieti, Ed. New York: Basic
        Books.
Frankl, Viktor E.
  1963 Man's Search for Meaning. New York: Washington
        Square Press.

1967   Psychotherapy and Existentialism: Selected Papers
       on Logotherapy. New York: Simon & Schuster.
1969   The Will to Meaning: Foundations and Applications
       of Logotherapy. New York: New American Library.
Furst, Peter T.
1973   The Roots and Continuities of Shamanism. Arts
       Canada. 30:33-60.
Gastaut, Henri, Roger, J., Corriol, J., and Y. Gastaut
1949   L'épilepsie induite par la stimulation auditive intermit-
       tente rhythmée ou épilepsie 'psophogénique'. EEG
       and Clinical Neurophysiology 1:121.
Goldman, D.
1952   The effect of rhythmic auditory stimulation on the
       human electroencephalogram. EEG and Clinical
       Neurophysiology 4:370.
Guariglia, Guglielmo
1959   Prophetismus und Heilserwartungs-Bewegungen als
       volkerkundliches und religionsgeschichtliches Problem.
       Horn, Austria: Berger.
Gunther, Erna
1927   Klallam Ethnography. University of Washington
       Publications in Anthropology 1/5. Seattle: University
       of Washington Press.
1949   The Shaker Religion of the Northwest. In Indians of
       the Urban Northwest, Marian W. Smith, Ed. New
       York: Columbia University Press.
Haeberlin, Hermann K.
1918   sbEtEtda'q, a shamanistic performance of the Coast
       Salish. American Anthropologist 20:249-257.
Haeberlin, Hermann K. and Erna Gunther
1924   Ethnographische Notizen über die Indianerstämme
       des Puget-Sundes. Zeitschrift für Ethnologie, Jahrgang
       1924. Pp. 1-74.
1930   The Indians of Puget Sound. University of Washing-

ton Publications in Anthropology 4/1. Seattle: University of Washington Press.

Hambly, W.D.
1926   Origins of Education Among Primitive Peoples. London: Macmillan.

Hill-Tout, Charles
1900   Notes on the Sk.qo'mic of British Columbia, a Branch of the Great Salish Stock of North America. Report of the 70th Meeting of the British Association for the Advancement of Science, 1900:472-549.

1901   The Origin of the Totemism of the Aborigines of British Columbia. Transactions of the Royal Society of Canada, Section 11:3-15.

1902   Ethnological Studies of the Mainland Halkomelem, A Division of the Salish of British Columbia. Report of the 72nd Meeting of the British Association for the Advancement of Science, 1902:355-449.

1904   Ethnological Report on the Stseelis and Skaulits Tribes of the Halkomelem Division of the Salish of British Columbia. Journal of the Royal Anthropological Institute of Great Britain and Ireland 34:311-376.

1905a   Report on the Ethnology of the Stlatlumh of British Columbia. Journal of the Royal Anthropological Institute of Great Britain and Ireland 35:126-218.

1905b   The Salish Tribes of the Coast and Lower Fraser Delta. Annual Archaeological Report of the Ontario Provincial Museum, 1905:225-235.

1907   British North America; The Far West, The Home of the Salish and Déné. London: Constable.

Hippler, Arthur
1980   Review of 'The Psychiatrist and his Shaman Colleague', by W. Jilek and L. Jilek-Aall. Transcultural Psychiatric Research Review 17:189-193.

Horney, Karen
1937   The Neurotic Personality of Our Time. New York: Norton.

Howard, J.H.
1976   The Plains Gourd Dance as a Revitalization Movement. American Ethnologist 3:243-259.

Hultkrantz, Åke
1953   Conceptions of the soul among North American Indians; a study in religious ethnology. The Ethnographical Museum of Sweden Monograph Series Publication No. 1. Stockholm: Caslon Press.

Huxley, Aldous
1961   The Devils of Loudun. London: Chatto and Windus.

Indian Health Service Task Force on Alcoholism
1969   Alcoholism, A High Priority Health Problem; Section 1. Washington: U.S. Department of Health, Education and Welfare.

Jenness, Diamond
1955   The Faith of a Coast Salish Indian. Anthropology in British Columbia Memoir 3. Victoria: Provincial Museum of British Columbia.

Jilek, Wolfgang G.
1971   From Crazy Witch Doctor to Auxiliary Psychotherapist, The Changing Image of the Medicine Man. Psychiatria Clinica 4:200-220.

1978   Native Renaissance: The Survival and Revival of Indigenous Therapeutic Ceremonials Among North American Indians. Transcultural Psychiatric Research Review 15:117-147.

Jilek, Wolfgang G., and Louise Jilek-Aall
1970   Transient Psychoses in Africans. Psychiatria Clinica 3:337-364.

1978   The Psychiatrist and his Shaman Colleague: Cross-Cultural Collaboration with Traditional Amerindian

169

Therapists. Journal of Operational Psychiatry 9:32-39.

Jilek, Wolfgang G., and Chunilal Roy
  1976 Homicide Committed by Canadian Indians and Non-Indians. International Journal of Offender Therapy and Comparative Criminology 20:201-216

Jilek, Wolfgang G., and Norman Todd
  1974 Witchdoctors Succeed Where Doctors Fail: Psychotherapy Among Coast Salish Indians. Canadian Psychiatric Association Journal 19:351-356.

Jilek-Aall, Louise M.
  1964 Geisteskrankheiten und Epilepsie im Tropischen Afrika. Fortschritte der Neurologie und Psychiatrie 32:213-259.

  1974 Psychosocial Aspects of Drinking Among Coast Salish Indians. Canadian Psychiatric Association Journal 19:357-361.

  1978 Alcohol and the Indian-White Relationship: A Study of the Function of Alcoholics Anonymous among Coast Salish Indians. Confinia Psychiatrica 21:195-233.

Jilek-Aall, Louise, Jilek, Wolfgang G., and Frank Flynn
  1978 Sex Role, Culture and Psychopathology: A Comparative Study of Three Ethnic Groups in Western Canada. Journal of Psychological Anthropology 1:473-488.

Jorgensen, Joseph G.
  1972 The Sun Dance Religion: Power for the Powerless. Chicago: University of Chicago Press.

Jung, Carl G.
  1952 Symbole der Wandlung. Zurich: Rascher.

Kasamatsu A., and T. Hirai
  1966 An Electroencephalographic Study on the Zen Meditation (Zazen). Folia Psychiatrica et Neurologica Japonica 20:315-336.

Kasamatsu, A., and Y. Shimazono
  1957 'Clinical Concept and Neurophysiological Basis of the Disturbance of Consciousness. Folia Psychiatrica et Neurologica Japonica 11:969-999.

Kew, John E. M.
  1970 Coast Salish Ceremonial Life; Status and Identity in a Modern Village. Doctoral Thesis, Dept. of Anthropology, University of Washington, Seattle.

Kluckhohn, Clyde
  1942 Myths and Rituals, a General Theory. The Harvard Theological Review 35:45-79.

Kroeber, Alfred L.
  1952 The Nature of Culture. Chicago: University of Chicago Press.

Kugler, Johann
  1966 Elektroencephalographie in Klinik und Praxis. Stuttgart: Thieme.

Lambo, T. Adeoye
  1956 Neuropsychiatric Observations in the Western Region of Nigeria. British Medical Journal ii:1388-1394.

Lane, Barbara S.
  1953 A Comparative and Analytical Study of some Aspects of Northwest Coast Religion. Doctoral Thesis, Dept. of Anthropology, University of Washington, Seattle.

LaViolette, Forrest E.
  1961 The Struggle for Survival; Indian Cultures and the Protestant Ethic in British Columbia. Toronto: University of Toronto Press.

Leighton, Dorothea C., J. S. Harding, D. B. Macklin, A. M. Macmillan, and A. H. Leighton
  1963 The Character of Danger. New York: Basic Books.

Leighton, Alexander H., R. Prince, R. May
  1968 The Therapeutic Process in Cross-Cultural Perspective; A Symposium. American Journal of Psychiatry 124:1171-1183.

171

Lemert, Edwin M.
  1955   The Life and Death of an Indian State. Human Organization 13:23-27.
Lerman, Norman H.
  1954   An Okanagan Winter Dance. *In* Anthropology in British Columbia 4., Wilson Duff, Ed. Victoria: Provincial Museum of British Columbia. (Provincial Museum Annual Report 4:35-36).
Lévi-Strauss, Claude
  1962   La pensée sauvage. Paris: Plon.
  1963   Structural Anthropology. New York: Basic Books.
  1975   La voie des masques, 2 vols. Geneva: Editions d'Art Albert Skira.
  1979   La voie des masques et Trois excursions. Paris: Plon.
Lindsley, D. B.
  1960   Attention, Consciousness, Sleep and Wakefulness. *In* Handbook of Physiology, Section 1: Neurophysiology 3., J. Field and H. W. Magoun, Eds. Washington: American Physiological Society.
Linton, Ralph
  1943   Nativistic Movements. American Anthropologist 45:230-240.
Loomis, A. L., E. N. Harvey, and G. Hobart
  1936   Electrical Potentials of the Human Brain. Journal of Experimental Psychology 19:249-279.
Ludwig, Arnold M.
  1968   Altered States of Consciousness. *In* Trance and Possession States, Raymond Prince, Ed. Montreal: R. M. Bucke Memorial Society.
Margetts, Edward L.
  1975   Canada: Indian and Eskimo medicine, with notes on the early history of psychiatry among French and British colonists. *In* World History of Psychiatry, John G. Howells, Ed. Pp. 400-431. New York: Brunner/Mazel.

Mauss, Marcel
1950   Sociologie et anthropologie. Paris: Presses Universitaires.

May, Philip A., and Larry H. Dizmang
1974   Suicide and the American Indian. Psychiatric Annals 4:22-28.

Merton, Robert K.
1938   Social Structure and Anomie. American Sociological Review 3:672-682.

Mooney, James
1896   The Ghost-Dance Religion and the Sioux Outbreak of 1890. Bureau of American Ethnology 14th Annual Report, 1892-93. Washington: U.S. Government Printing Office.

Moreno, Jacob L.
1923   Das Stegreiftheater. Berlin: Kiepenheuer.

1955   The Significance of the Therapeutic Format and the Place of Acting Out in Psychotherapy. Group Psychotherapy 8:7-21.

1959   Psychodrama. In American Handbook of Psychiatry 2., Silvano Arieti, Ed. New York: Basic Books.

Mumford. Lewis
1951   The Conduct of Life. New York: Harcourt.

Neher, A.
1961   Auditory Driving observed with Scalp Electrodes in Normal Subjects. EEG and Clinical Neurophysiology 13:449-451.

1962   A Physiological Explanation of Unusual Behaviour in Ceremonies Involving Drums. Human Biology 34:151-160.

Olson, Ronald L.
1936   The Quinault Indians. University of Washington Publications in Anthropology 6/1. Seattle: University of Washington Press.

Paracelsus (Theophrastus von Hohenheim)
1933   Labyrinthus medicorum errantium. Sämtliche Werke
11., K. Sudhoff, Ed. Munich: Alber.

Parsons, Talcott
1949   The Structure of Social Action 1. New York: Free
Press.
1951   The Social System. New York: Free Press.

Prince, Raymond
1968   Can the EEG be used in the Study of Possession
States? *In* Trance and Possession States, Raymond
Prince, Ed. Montreal: R. M. Bucke Memorial Society.

Ray, Verne F.
1932   The Sanpoil and Nespelem. University of Washington Publications in Anthropology 5. Seattle: University of Washington Press.
1939   Cultural Relations in the Plateau of Northwestern
America. Publications of the Frederick Webb Hodge
Anniversary Publications Fund. Los Angeles: South-
west Museum.
1942   Culture elements distributions XXII: Plateau. Anthropological Records Vol. 8. No. 2. Berkeley: University
of California Press.

Robbins, Rossell H.
1959   The Encyclopedia of Witchcraft and Demonology.
New York: Crown.

Robinson, Sarah A.
1963   Spirit Dancing Among the Salish Indians, Vancouver
Island, British Columbia. Doctoral Thesis, Dept of
Anthropology, University of Chicago, Chicago.

Rodewyk, Adolf, S. J.
1963 . Die Daemonische Besessenheit in der Sicht des Rituale
Romanum. Aschaffenburg: Pattloch.

Roy, Chunilal, Adjit Choudhuri, and Donald Irvine
1970   The Prevalence of Mental Disorders Among Saskat-

chewan Indians. Journal of Cross-Cultural Psychology 1:383-392.

Sahagún, Fray Bernardino de
1977   Historia General de las Cosas de Nueva España, 1st ed. 1560. (Vol. 3, Book 11, Chapter 7). Mexico: Editorial Porrua.

Sargant, William
1959   Battle for the Mind. London: Pan Books.

1967   Witch Doctoring, Zar and Voodoo: Their Relation to Modern Psychiatric Treatments. Proceedings of the Royal Society, Medicine 60:1055-1060.

Schilder, Paul
1953   Medical Psychology. New York: International University Press.

Schlesinger, Benno
1962   Higher Cerebral Functions and Their Clinical Disorders; The Organic Basis of Psychology and Psychiatry. New York: Grune and Stratton.

Schmitt, N., L. W. Hole and W. S. Barclay
1966   Accidental Deaths Among British Columbia Indians. Canadian Medical Association Journal 94:228-234.

Schwimmer, E. G.
1970   Symbolic Competition. Paper presented at a Symposium on Canadian Indian Social Organization, Winnipeg, May 1970. Typescript 47pp.

Smith, Marian W.
1938   MS notes from 1938 field trip. *Cited in* Helen Codere, The Swai'xwe myth of the Middle Fraser River: the integration of two Northwest Coast cultural ideas. Pp. 2-4. Journal of American Folklore. 61:1-18.

1940   The Puyallup-Nisqually. New York: Columbia University Press.

Spier, Leslie
1930   Klamath Ethnography. University of California Pub-

lications in American Archaeology and Ethnology 30. Berkeley/Los Angeles: University of California Press.

1953   The Prophet Dance of the Northwest and its Derivatives; The Source of the Ghost Dance. Menasha, Wisconsin: Banta.

Spradley, James P.
1953   The Kwakiutl Guardian Spirit Quest, An Historical, Functional and Comparative Analysis. Master of Arts Thesis, Dept. of Anthropology, University of Washington, Seattle.

Stern, Bernhard J.
1934   The Lummi Indians of Northwest Washington. New York: Columbia Unviersity Press.

Suttles, Wayne
1954   Post-Contact Culture Change Among the Lummi Indians. The British Columbia Historical Quarterly 18:29-102.

1955   Katzie Ethnographic Notes. Anthropology in British Columbia Memoir 2. Victoria: Provincial Museum of British Columbia.

1957   The Plateau Prophet Dance Among the Coast Salish. Southwestern Journal of Anthropology 13:352-396.

1963   The Persistence of Intervillage Ties Among the Coast Salish. Ethnology 2:512-525.

Teit, James
1900   The Thompson Indians of British Columbia. Memoirs of the American Museum of Natural History 2./ Anthropology 1/ The Jesup North Pacific Expedition 4. New York: American Museum of Natural History.

1905   The Shuswap. Memoir of the American Museum of Natural History 2./The Jesup North Pacific Expedition 7. New York: American Museum of Natural History.

1930   The Salishan Tribes of the Western Plateaus. Bureau

of American Ethnology 45 Annual Report, 1927-28.
Washington: U.S. Government Printing Office.

Titeca, J., and J. Kluyskens
1962 Etude électroencéphalographique des altérations du
champ visuel induites par hypnose. Bulletin, Aca-
démie royale de Médecine Belg. 7:413-441.

Van der Walde, Peter H.
1965 Interpretation of Hypnosis in Terms of Ego Psychology. Archives of General Psychiatry 12:438-447.

1968 Trance States and Ego Psychology. *In* Trance and
Possession States, Raymond Prince, Ed. Montreal:
R. M. Bucke Memorial Society.

Vorländer, Karl
1923 Geschichte der Philosophie. Berlin: Kiepenheuer.

Wallace, Anthony F. C.
1956 Revitalization Movements. American Anthropologist 58:264-281.

Walter, V. J., and W. Grey Walter
1949 The Central Effects of Rhythmic Sensory Stimulation. EEG and Clinical Neurophysiology 1:57-86.

Waterman, T. T.
1930 The paraphernalia of the Duwamish "Spirit-Canoe"
ceremony. Indian Notes 7:129-148, 295-312, 535-561.
New York: Museum of the American Indian, Heye
Foundation.

Wickersham, James
1898 Nusqually mythology: studies of the Washington
Indians. Overland Monthly 32:345-351.

Wike, Joyce A.
1941 Modern Spirit Dancing of Northern Puget Sound.
Master of Arts Thesis, Dept. of Anthropology,
University of Washinton, Seattle.

Willard, William
1979 American Indians. *In* Suicide: Theory and Clinical
Aspects, L. D. Hankoff, Ed. Littleton, Mass.: PSG
Publishing.

Willoughby, C.

1889   Indians of the Quinaielt Agency, Washington Territory. *In* Annual Report of the Board of Regents of the Smithsonian Institution for the year ending June 30, 1886. Part 2:267-282. Washington: Government Printing Office.

Wilson, Capt. E. E.

1866   Report on the Indian Tribes Inhabiting the Country in the Vicinity of the 49th Parallel of North Latitude. Transactions of the Ethnological Society of London 4:275-332.

Wingert, Paul S.

1949   American Indian sculpture: a study of the Northwest Coast. New York: J. J. Augustin.

Wissler, Clark

1931   The American Indian. New York: Oxford University Press.

Wittkower, Eric D.

1970   Trance and Possession States. The International Journal of Social Psychiatry 16:153-160.

Yap, P. M.

1960   The Possession Syndrome, a Comparison of Hong Kong and French Findings. Journal of Mental Science 106:114-137.

Glossary

abreactive	adjective pertaining to cathartic abreaction (q.v.).
acoustic or auditory driving	specific patterning of the electroencephalogram ("brain waves") due to the effects of acoustic stimulation of a particular stimulus frequency and intensity.
analgesia	insensibility to pain.
anorectic	adjective pertaining to anorexia (q.v.).
anorexia	loss of appetite.
cathartic abreaction	re-living and re-enacting of repressed experiences with appropriate emotional expression and discharge.
cholecystitis	inflammatory disease process affecting the gall-bladder.
dysphoric	adjective pertaining to dysphoria; an emotional state characterised by feelings of listlessness, sadness, discomfort and anxiety.
dyspnea	difficulty of breathing.
edematous	adjective pertaining to edema; a swelling due to retention of watery fluid in the intercellular spaces of connective tissues.
forced hypermotility	a state of rapid active motion imposed on the individual.
gustatory	pertaining to the sense of taste.
hypnagogic	pertaining to experiences occuring on the edge of sleep; such as visual hallucinations or illusions, most often experienced by normal persons during periods of anxiety and tension.

179

hypnopompic	pertaining to experiences occuring on the edge of waking; such as transient persistence of dream imagery though the eyes are open.
hypoxaemia	reduced oxygenation (i.e., charging with oxygen) of the blood.
olfactory	pertaining to the sense of smell.
pathognomonic	specifically characteristic symptom indicative of a particular disease.
pathoplastic	pertaining to the influence on symptom formation exercised by environmental (largely socio-cultural) factors which shape the presented disease phenomena without having caused them.
photic driving	specific patterning of the electroencephalogram ("brain waves") due to the effects of light stimulation of a particular stimulus frequency and intensity, e.g., by a stroboscopic flicker light apparatus as used in laboratories of electroencephalography.
photogenic epilepsy	epileptic seizures triggered by intermittent flicker light stimulation; e.g., by stroboscopic photostimulation (q.v.) under laboratory conditions, or by exposure to other sources of flickering light (fire; sunlight interrupted by passing fence, etc.).
proprioceptive stimuli	stimuli arising from the observer's own organism.
psychohygienic	pertaining to actions which directly or indirectly effect the maintenance of emotional balance and the prevention of mental, psychosomatic and psycho-social malfunction and disorder, and which facilitate the individual's positive adaptation to its social and physical environment. Actions with intended or unintended psychohygienic effects can be taken on the individual or societal level.

180

psychotherapeutic	**adjective** pertaining to psychotherapy: methods of treating ill health which are based on psychological rather than physical or chemical techniques. Psychotherapy may be undertaken individually or as group therapy. Methods include supportive psychotherapy with guidance, reassurance and direct ego support; suggestive ("faith healing") and hypnotic techniques; cathartic abreaction; psychodrama; behaviour and conditioning therapies; psychoanalysis and existential analysis of various schools. The maximal aim of psychotherapy is a reorientation of the patient's personality.
stroboscopic photostimulation	exposure to the effects of the flicker light apparatus which produces light flashes of varying frequencies by periodic interruption of the beam. Used in electroencephalographic examinations for its specific effects on the electric potentials of the brain as recorded in the EEG (electroencephalogram) for diagnostic purposes.
sudorific	causing heavy perspiration.
synaesthetic	adjective pertaining to synaesthesia; a sensation experienced in one sense modality by a stimulus applied to a different sense modality; e.g., a sensation of colours when music is heard.

Acknowledgments

I am grateful to my Indian friends Chief Richard Malloway and Mr. Roy Point of Sardis, B.C., Mr. Isadore Tom and Mr. Joe Washington of Lummi, Washington, and Mr. Walker Stogan of Musqueam, B.C., who invited me to attend at ceremonial occasions as a guest and to assist as a witness. I have learned to respect these Indian elders for their warm humanity and devotion to their people, and for the keen psychological insight they displayed. It is their hope that a better understanding of the ceremonial by health professionals and social scientists, may lead to a full appreciation of its merits.

No useful purpose would be served by always revealing the identity of an Indian person when presenting in this book the information he or she contributed. In order to safeguard anonymity, references to personal characteristics are kept at a minimum, and coded initials are employed in the text.

I shall remain indebted to the late Professor Wilson Duff and to Professor David F. Aberle, Ph.D., of the Department of Anthropology and Sociology, University of British Columbia, for their valuable advice. The formulations and conclusions in Chapter Eleven of this book owe much to stimulating discussions with Professor Claude Lévi-Strauss during his visits to British Columbia. In my transcultural psychiatric work with indigenous populations, I have always been encouraged by my esteemed teacher and dear friend, Professor Manfred Bleuler of Zurich, a champion of the noble cause of protecting the habitat and environment of people who respect Nature against those who recklessly exploit it. Finally, I remember with gratitude that in rendering psychiatric services to the Indian people, I was always able to rely on the assistance of my wife, Dr. Louise Jilek-Aall, and of my physician-friend Dr. Norman Todd, from Chilliwack, B.C. Together we have pioneered the practice of close medical cooperation with traditional Indian therapists for the benefit of our Indian patients.

THIS BOOK IS DEDICATED TO LOUISE AND TO OUR INDIAN FRIENDS